A Redemption Song

A Redemption Song

Illuminations on Black British Pastoral Theology

Delroy Hall

scm press

© Delroy Hall 2021

Published in 2021 by SCM Press
Editorial office
3rd Floor, Invicta House,
108–114 Golden Lane,
London EC1Y 0TG, UK

www.scmpress.co.uk

SCM Press is an imprint of Hymns Ancient & Modern Ltd
(a registered charity)

Hymns Ancient & Modern® is a registered trademark of
Hymns Ancient & Modern Ltd
13A Hellesdon Park Road, Norwich,
Norfolk NR6 5DR, UK

British Library Cataloguing in Publication data

A catalogue record for this book is available
from the British Library

ISBN 978-0-334-06072-7

Typeset by Regent Typesetting
Printed and bound by
CPI Group (UK) Ltd

Contents

Acknowledgements

As is often said, books are never the effort of only one person. The contributions from a myriad of people have knowingly and unknowingly been part of the development of this publication.

I must acknowledge the ambition and love of my parents: my mother Dorothy, who remains fiercely independent at the age of 86, and my father Lindo, who passed away over 30 years ago at the young age of 52. They met here in the UK, having travelled from the Caribbean in the early fifties, and married in 1957 in Newark, Nottingham. I did not realize at the time that they were both bright, sharp and ambitious people who did not have the privilege of much education beyond school in Jamaica.

In his late twenties, my father was ready to relocate to Canada, where builder's joiners were needed for the construction industry. Through a series of events, my parents changed their minds and headed for Leicester, where I remained until 1996.

I must also thank fellow sojourners along my academic pathway. Delroy Reid Salmon, who now as best friend has given intellectual encouragement and been a challenger to academic and ministerial development.

Thanks go to Eric Williams, fellow academic warrior who, along with his gift of finding excellent places to eat, is seriously sharp at creating and finding catchy titles for pieces of writing.

I must also thank, albeit posthumously, the late Caroline Redfern and Lynnette Mullings, who were developing scholars during their time at the University of Birmingham as they worked through their doctoral studies. Sadly both succumbed

vii

to the dreaded pang of cancer literally days away from submission and never completed their theses. Had they submitted their theses, passed their vivas and published, they would have made necessary and substantial dents in the area of Black theology, sexuality and womanist perspectives within the Black Majority Church on the UK landscape. Black Majority Church is where the ethnic majority membership of the church is black, rather than the leadership.

A latecomer to my academic life, with a recommendation from Eric Williams, is Fred Ware, Associate Dean for Academic Affairs at Howard University School of Divinity. Being unsure how to lay out the various chapters for this book, I emailed him for help and he suggested I send him the chapter outlines. We met at Howard University and his suggested layout for these apparently odd writing projects was creative, gave clear structure and helped me value and appreciate the work I had written.

The person who has challenged me the most to write and been a constant loving 'flea in my ear' has been Anthony Reddie, who has unselfishly offered support, encouragement and time to the book. Already he is prodding me in the direction of a second book. A challenge I have already taken on board.

One person I cannot forget is Inderjit Bhogle, who, through eons of me asking how to do theological reflections, has taught me a method that has stayed with me ever since. Thank you.

I cannot forget my sister Sandra, who with a sharp mind has always been a supporter of my development. The final supports to my writing development are my wife Paulette and my twin daughters Saffron and Jordan, who would not take it too lightly if I introduced them as my girls as they are now women in their mid-twenties and have their own opinions and thoughts about things.

I have enjoyed reading, re-working and editing each chapter. I hope you too will enjoy reading it while asking critical questions which will only serve to improve what has been written.

Introduction

Fifty years after first wanting to write a book, here it is. My desire to write a book, or books even, began as a 14 year old who loved composition, as it was called in those days. Using one's creative imagination to write a story. After having a story read in class by the English teacher and having two short stories published in the school newsletter, I wanted to write thriller novels, but I did not know the process of writing a book. After six years of repeatedly trying, I quit. Not only did I not know how to write a book, I also concluded that Black people never wrote books, so what was the point? I now know that my earlier conclusions were untrue and I now know that books are written one word, one sentence, one paragraph, one section and one chapter at a time with structure and a plan of sorts.

What follows are my intellectual and pastoral musings on the life and plight of my African ancestors, who were enslaved during the transatlantic slave trade, and the Windrush generation and their subsequent offspring in the UK. At the time of writing these various articles, I had not envisaged that they would form a collection leading to a seminal text on a Black British pastoral theology.

Chapter 1 captures my reflections on how I position myself as a Black man in Britain and on being perceived by others as a problem. I am one of few Black male Caribbean counsellors in the UK. Furthermore, this chapter positions me as a Black human being, a Christian pastor, trainer and trained psychotherapist who happens to be born in England and initially was oblivious to the history surrounding my cultural heritage. While my life journey is unique, as are all our life's journeys, it also mirrors that of countless African Caribbean people born in the UK, the mother country, during the late 1950s and 1960s. I was born here and this is where I call home, sort of. I am meant to be a part of British society, but I stand out visibly and I am reminded daily that I am different. Despite standing out and being a target for discrimination, Black people remain resilient. At times, against the odds.

Chapter 2 provides the historical context of how Africans arrived in the Americas. There is a commonly-held view that all Black people are the same. That is, Africans and African Caribbeans are all one and the same. This is due to immense societal pressure for homogeneity and assimilation. For me, the crucial distinction between continental Africans and African Caribbean people is the horrendous journey from Africa to the Americas called the Middle Passage. This terrifying and miserable sojourn was the transportation of human cargo from Africa to the Americas and was the middle leg of trade. The first leg of the journey carried material possessions from the UK to be traded for African slaves. The final part of the journey was ships laden with sugar, cotton and tobacco, lucrative bounty fortifying Britain's Industrial Revolution. It must be emphasized: the Africans did not apply for jobs to relocate to the Americas. Neither were they on holiday or on secondment. They were enslaved and, in becoming so, they were deprived of everything imaginable about their identity and their humanity into being nobodies. In sociological terms they were objectified, in a business sense they were commodified as chattels for insurance purposes; and in a human sense they were dehumanized. The Middle Passage is seen through the lens of the Easter story of Crucifixion, Holy Saturday and Resurrection. Needless to say, this was a trek of existential consequence.

Following on from the chapter describing the Middle Passage, Chapter 3 engages the Eucharist and gives the opportunity for suffering to speak as a precursor to liberation. The Eucharist, having its genesis in the deliverance of the Israelites centuries before, via the Passover Lamb in Egypt, and now instituted by Jesus, provides a means for human suffering to be acknowledged, voiced and heard while heading for healing and liberation. Here we focus on the life of Sam Sharpe, Baptist deacon and the main contributor, as far as Caribbeans are concerned, to ending the slave trade in Jamaica. Sharp is featured for mobilizing the enslaved, through the use of Bible studies and prayer meetings, into action for their liberation. The eucharistic sacrament is used as a point of theological reflection in understanding the life of Sam Sharpe and in developing a paradigm for ministerial practice in the twenty-first century.

The eucharistic theme is continued as a mysterious meal for all people. Chapter 4 looks at the often-unspoken violence surrounding the origins of the meal, with the Passover Lamb in Egypt, and the violence surrounding the meal Jesus instituted. While Christians throughout the world gather at various times to partake in the Holy Communion, a case is developed for this act of eating the Lord's body and drinking his blood being also a means of healing. The focus of this chapter is how the meal can be interpreted for African Caribbean diasporan people in dealing with intergenerational trauma, marginalization and discrimination. However, its wider appeal is for all human beings, all flawed and broken and in need of healing. Participating in the Holy Communion is a way for healing to begin and continue.

Chapter 5 interrogates how Black people are perceived, described and labelled by the Western psyche. The importance of names and their linkage to identity is examined. For many cultures names have huge and significant meanings, while labelling someone is, implicitly, referring to them as a thing, an object and most definitely not human. Labels are placed on packages and names are given to human beings. While negative labelling has not been developed by Black people, they are left with the ontological task of renaming themselves to create a life in which they value who they are within a society still wrestling with Blackness and how Black people can be seen as equals.

Chapter 6 continues the quest for Black people, with an emphasis on Black men developing a theological paradigm for self-love. Black men in Western society occupy a dangerous place created not by them but by the minds of White women and men alike. Black men are simultaneously sexualized and exoticized by White women and White gay men, and are the target of extreme violence by White men, as exemplified by the killing of George Floyd in America and the high proportion of Black men who are assaulted by police and incarcerated by the prison industry in both America and the UK.

Black men cannot wait for legislation and the West to reappraise itself and make the necessary adjustments for racial equality. Black men must recover from the 'dis-ease' of self-loathing, developed over centuries of violent humiliation and living within structures where they are still seen as a problem. They must learn to face reality, walk away from victimhood and rehumanize themselves to reach their potential and to function in ways that are wholesome and satisfying. The work needed is not found in the self-help sections in many bookstores, but it must be radical in being independent of White validation.

Chapter 7 continues with the theme of Black autonomy within a White context. Drawing on the work, origins and purpose of Black theology, it stresses that Black liberation theology should not break its neck seeking acceptance in the halls of White academia. It is a theology pronouncing the liberation of Black people, while recognizing that in the battle of the oppressed and oppressor there are no winners. All are dehumanized in the process and all need liberating. Gaining access to White academia will only serve to weaken its potency by confining its emphasis on speaking truth to power within a context where the indigenous population still has huge difficulty in talking about race, injustice and inequality. The major difficulty is that a vocabulary for discussing such complexities is yet to be developed and, while there is pressure for homogenization and assimilation, such a language will never be established if conversation does not take place. The conversation of race and how it can be developed is an excellent proposal, but growth will not progress if people are not prepared to listen and hear each other speak.

The final chapter offers a trajectory that a Black British pastoral theology must travel if it is going to speak to the people within and without the walls of security of the Church.

At the end of each chapter, you will find 'Questions for Further Reflection'. These can be used alone or in a group, and are designed to clarify or expand your thinking about the issues raised.

The Effects of an African Caribbean Heritage: Living as a Problem

Introduction

The phrase 'what you see is what you get' is not always true. In this chapter I will sketch some of the darker, untold and unacknowledged aspects of African Caribbean life. The term 'African Caribbean' charts a specific group of people: those whose cultural history includes the horrendous sojourn of the Middle Passage – a subject to which I will refer later in the chapter.

While writing, I run the risk of being classed as the stereo-typical angry Black man. However, I will leave the reader to make their decision. Angry or not, this is a view of an African Caribbean man in understanding the effects of an African Caribbean heritage of living as a problem within British society.

Heritage and its various meanings

What is heritage and who decides what it comprises? As a simple word with multiple meanings, heritage refers to some-thing that is handed down from a previous generation and, as argued by Peter Howard (2003), it is those things people want to save, collect or conserve. Heritage is recognized, designated and self-conscious by definition. Emphasizing its importance, Helaine Silverman and D. Fairchild Ruggles (2007) argue that heritage should be ranked equal to human rights because as a concept it demands that individual and group identities be respected and protected. Furthermore, they stress that heritage insists on the recognition of a person's or community's essential worth. Heritage, then, relates to human existence and significance. The inclusion of human significance is a major development with concerns about monuments, historic sites and buildings. For this chapter I will use Brian Graham and Peter Howard's understanding of heritage, recognizing the complex linkage it has with identity. Using a 'constructionist position, they conceptualize heritage as referring to the ways in which selective past material artefacts, natural landscapes, mythologies, memories, and traditions become cultural, political and economic resources for the present' (Graham and Howard, 2008, p. 2). What is of social worth to a specific group of people cannot always be understood by outsiders of the cultural group. Furthermore, there is danger when one cultural heritage considers itself more superior than others. Describing an African Caribbean heritage is complicated.

African Caribbean heritage

For African Caribbean people living in British society there is a contextual similarity to the time when W. E. B. Du Bois wrote *The Souls of Black Folk* (1994). He was asked, 'How does it feel to be a problem?' This labelling was not an incidental moment in the lives of African Americans in early twentieth-century America but is the daily experience of most African diaspora people. One never acclimatizes to this way of life but learns to live painfully with it; however, an anecdotal account illustrating a counter narrative may be helpful.

In May 2010, I presented a paper at the Caribbean Studies Association in Barbados. Before the conference started, I rested for a few days and had an unusual experience which needed exploring. After quite some time of reflection it became evident why I had sensed this unfamiliar freedom. First, I was with Black people, and I was one with the dominant population.

Second, I felt connected to the land even though my parents were of Jamaican heritage. I had never felt such psychological/ existential liberation in England, the land of my birth. This experience, while not the focus for analysis, serves to highlight the plight of many African Caribbean people living in Britain as being somewhat estranged.

It must be emphasized that 'an' African Caribbean, or 'the' African Caribbean heritage does not exist. The Caribbean is not a homogenous group of islands or a people group. Each island has areas of particularity and its own peculiarity. One of the common features comprising African Caribbean heritage is the legacy of the institution of enslavement. Slavery permeated the whole of the Caribbean, but the island exhibiting the most symptoms of enslavement is Jamaica (Fletchman Smith, 2000). The violent past began in 1492 when Christopher Columbus arrived in the West Indies (Grant, 2007). While praising his expeditions, the history on Columbus often omits the elimination of the Arawak Indians, the natives of Jamaica (The Gleaner, 1995). Through history, and with various nations fighting for control of Jamaica and other Caribbean islands coupled with the institution of enslavement and empire, Jamaica experienced gratuitous forms of violence for over 500 years; hence, it seems logical that behaviour concomitant with a history of conflict, violence, subjugation, exploitation and extreme suffering would transpire. Thus, it is argued that the protracted process of dehumanization affected the enslaved on the plantations and subsequent generations right to the present day (Akbar, 1996).

Enslaved Africans were 'drafted' in to work the plantations and were then laid off by the abolition of slavery, due not so much to William Wilberforce but more to the fight for liberation led by Baptist deacon Sam Sharpe (Dick, 2009). The abolition of slavery rendered the enslaved redundant, without a welfare package.

African Caribbean heritage: the makeup of myths and stories is exoticized through the lens of excellent cuisine and music, in particular reggae, calypso and the steel pans, and by dance, fashion and literature. But the underbelly of African Caribbean life is demonized, marginalized and counts for nothing. The question remains: given its horrific history, is it possible for a heritage to exist?

The existence of African Caribbean heritage

Heritage, whether good or bad, is heritage. The possibility of a heritage is similar to the question asked by African American historian John Henrik Clarke when as a boy he told his schoolteacher he wanted to learn about Black people's history. He was told in no uncertain terms that Black people did not have a history or a culture (Clarke, 1998) – a belief still held by many today (James, 2020). What must be vehemently argued is that if there are people existing today, then a heritage must be present that has passed through previous generations. If heritage is the transmission of the essentials of life vital for ontological existence, then an African Caribbean heritage exists that includes the historical effects of conflict, violence and dehumanization. The continual mistreatment has become a part of the African Caribbean psyche that has attached itself like a limpet influencing Caribbean life and culture. The effects of this will take up the rest of this chapter.

The effects of an African Caribbean heritage

It is not possible to exoticize all Caribbean life. The problem with 'exoticization', the 'charm of the unfamiliar to the eyes of Europeans' (Rousseau and Porter, 1990), is that it fails to consider the brutal Caribbean past that renders national healing almost impossible. The question must be asked, 'Is there a need for clinicians to have an awareness of the effects of the African Caribbean legacy on its descendants today?' Having an awareness of the history is insufficient. Colin Lago, counsellor and supervisor, commenting from a counselling context, asserts that many counselling approaches focus on the present, but it must be recognized that a relevant understanding of history is necessary to understand current events (Lago and Thompson, 1996). While there is a phenomenon called empathy, it is almost impossible for people of the host population to empathetically comprehend the depth of pain, trauma and suffering of people living in a civilization that was not created for them. As an outsider you can conceptualize oppression but not experience it. The Caribbean proverb 'He who feels it knows it' is apt. Race awareness training comes a poor second in attempting to help non-Black people understand the dynamics of race and the experience of being Black.

The history of the dehumanization of African Caribbean people has been detrimental and the effects are still not fully known. A negative psychological effect of a Caribbean heritage is one of self-loathing. Self-hatred is a destructive by-product of hundreds of years of enslavement, when the black body was simultaneously an instrument of torture and a receptacle of European projection.

Leaving aside for a moment the physical brutality of enslavement, colonialism also must be considered as another form of dehumanization. Just as enslavement was appropriating black bodies as objects of property to produce sugar (Patterson, 1969), so colonialism was the commandeering of the property and minds of African Caribbean people. The capturing of African Caribbean people took place under British rule, and created an unconscious veiling of the Black self. I spoke recently with an African Caribbean woman in her mid-eighties who migrated to England in the early 1960s. She commented, 'We were born in Jamaica, but we never knew Jamaica.'[1]

The arrival in sunny Britain

During the 'Windrush' epoch, migrants arrived in Britain with a strong desire to embrace English values (Banton, 1953). England, in the Caribbean, was described as the 'Mother Country, where the streets were paved with gold' and was the Promised Land. African Caribbean people were schooled in the belief that they would be welcomed, embraced, and accepted as children of the Empire. In the main, this never happened. The rejection of African Caribbean migrants and their subsequent labelling as a societal problem is well-documented (Beckford, 1998). Gus John (1976) makes it clear that the negative response highlighted fissures and weakness within British society. In highlighting the fracture in British society, Kenneth Leech (2006) argued that the British government had a real opportunity to educate the nation on race relations but caused greater exclusion and demonization with the development and implementation of the 1968 Race Act.

Another effect of an African Caribbean heritage is historical amnesia. Many African Caribbean people living in Britain do not know who they are. There is often marginal or no knowledge of an African or Caribbean history. Many African Caribbean people have accepted the exoticization of their islands without any consideration of its past. A stark analogy with African Caribbean people not knowing who they are is that of adopted children who were never told about their adoption. One day, during adulthood and searching through old papers in the attic, they discover, to their dismay, that they were adopted. Other people knew important, personal and intimate details about their existence, but they did not. Some African Caribbean people sense that something is not right, but opt to ignore their existential rumblings because their current life is comfortable, so why rock the boat? For some, the uncovering of the past is too painful, so best leave it alone. The fact remains that most African Caribbean people of a certain generation can only trace back as far as their great-grandparents at best – or at worst. If mass historical amnesia exists, what are the psychological, emotional and existential consequences for people who cannot lay claim to their unique history? Marcus Garvey's comment is noteworthy here. He writes, 'A people without the knowledge of their past, history or origins is like a tree without roots.' Garvey's philosophical analogy contains much truth and indirectly suggests another dimension. If an observer ignores or denies the plant, they invariably deny the existence of the roots of that plant. Paul Grant uses similar language in supporting Garvey's comments. He states, 'If you don't know where you are going any road will do, and if you don't know your culture any culture will do' (2007). This historical memory loss leads to another danger.

Failure to examine or attempt to understand the extensive historical and intergenerational trauma of a people group often leads to inappropriate and ineffective treatment in the restoration and rehabilitation of African Caribbean people who suffer from an array of mental illnesses. There is always danger in only considering the present. Of course, it is possible to talk of awareness of the different other, but what effect does 'an awareness' play in affecting or influencing the methods of diagnosis, which are Eurocentric constructs assuming universal applicability? An example illustrates the partial inadequacy of Eurocentric concepts. Some years ago, I was in conversation with Emmanuel Lartey, a Ghanaian pastoral theologian who at the time was a senior lecturer in pastoral theology at the University of Birmingham, UK. As we spoke about mental illness and the impact of culture, he said that someone from Africa is at a huge disadvantage being in Britain in terms of cultural understanding, 'because what is understood as normal behaviour in Uganda is perceived as abnormal behaviour in the UK'.[2] He continued by saying it is normal for a young person in Africa, in their twenties, to remain at home, but in the UK such behaviour is generally misinterpreted as an individual with attachment issues.[3]

In treating African Caribbean clients, the diagnostic process must include an understanding of their collective history, even if the patient/client does not subscribe to or know anything about their cultural history. It is unfortunate, but the fact remains that in the twenty-first century with all its 'mod cons' to make life comfortable, we remain plagued with derogatory ideology about race (Grant, 2007). Highlighting the detrimental way in which non-White people are described, Cornel West (2002) speaks of the notion 'that Black people being human beings is a relatively new discovery in the modern West'. The difficulty in the discourse on race is coupled with the visible 'uncomfortableness' of talking about such matters. Similarly, the muting of one's voice or opinion is not a new strategy.

On the conscious and unconscious muting of the Black voice, Anthony Reddie (2006) comments that a Black person is rendered voiceless when their experiences, history and ongoing reality are ignored, disparaged or ridiculed. Thus the strategies of silencing and rendering one powerless are not those of physical violence, but violence in the form of mind games while continuing the propagation of White hegemony. Paul Grant (2007) cogently argues that psychological techniques are used more readily than the machinery of violence to pacify the Afrikans. By the term Afrikan with a 'k', Grant means people of African descent engaged with the struggle against oppression. The negation of African Caribbean life further compounds the feelings of disempowerment and marginalization leading to other detrimental effects of a turbulent history, as the following point demonstrates.

One of the most damaging features of an African Caribbean heritage is the breakdown of African Caribbean families in the UK. The instability of many African Caribbean families in the diaspora is not a problem that can be easily – if ever – unravelled. If the current trend of breakdown continues, the future for African Caribbean families in the UK looks bleak. Much of the evidence is supported by Robin Mann's research (Mann, 2009). Mann's work, while useful, fails to examine the historical context of how African families were disrupted during enslavement, the consequences of which the community is still grappling with today. The breakdown of African Caribbean families on another level signifies major problems in relationship building; however, this was not always the case.

Olaudah Equiano (2009) commented on how marriage and family life were culturally honoured dimensions of African life, but African life became fractured during enslavement. Anthony Pinn (2003) describes in graphic detail how the structure of African families was destroyed on the auction block during slavery. Pinn asserts: 'It did not take much imagination to recognize the traumatic experience the auction block entailed – separation from family, intrusive inspections and travels to new regions of the country and unfamiliar environments.' Thus the African family became a distorted configuration of the life that had sustained African civilizations for centuries. On the plantations, African family life was heavily scrutinized by the slave masters and was only encouraged as a means of providing extra labour for economic purposes. Emotional, psychological, spiritual and relational links were severed and this inevitably contributed to extending a life of suffering.

Black suffering – an existential crucifixion

Existential crucifixion, an idea first developed by Charles Cosgrove (1988, p. 179), referring to a dying with Christ, is used and reconfigured by me referring to a death of the self. The African Caribbean heritage of brutality, the decimation of Black life for the benefit of European profit, and the denial of one's humanity are a crucifixion of the Black self. Metaphorically speaking, crucifixion began with the capture of Africans for the transatlantic slave trade, continued during colonialism and arguably still exists in modern life. Existential crucifixion, a death of the self, has travelled with people of African Caribbean descent as an unwelcome parasitic enemy for centuries. Other marginalized groups also suffer, but there is a particular reference to people of African Caribbean and African American descent due to the historic episode in the formation of the Americas.

The Middle Passage, as mentioned earlier, was the horrific transhipment of human cargo from Africa to the Americas via the Atlantic in one of the worst protracted episodes of human misery and mistreatment ever recorded. It is estimated that approximately 12 million Africans were inhumanely shipped across the Atlantic on slave ships intentionally constructed to carry as many enslaved as possible (Gomez, 2005, p. 72). The 'tight packing' was a means of maximizing the limited space on the ships, but it led to major health problems. It is impossible to imagine the depth of human despair, misery and suffering experienced on the slave ships, but Michael Gomez attempts to capture the magnitude of human tragedy when he writes that 'The stench of the ships was so overpowering that

* Breaking the family and taking away what it meant to be a part of a tribe.

it could be scented for miles and the slave deck so covered with blood and mucus it resembled a slaughterhouse' (2005, p. 79). With such an impact on the existence and health of the enslaved, it mattered not if they died en route because they were considered chattels, and whatever was lost at sea would be compensated for by the insurance company as loss of property. The brutal journey from Africa to the Americas so traumatized the human cargo that many surviving the journey arrived in the Americas insane (Gomez, 2005, pp. 78–9). Anne Bailey (2007), describing the Middle Passage, employs the term 'terror', indicating that terror is designed to harm its objects physically and psychologically.

From the terror of the Middle Passage, dislocation and displacement from their homeland to another country, the enslaved Africans experienced an existential crucifixion. I admit that this concept is difficult to define but suggest that existential crucifixion includes the moment when the enslaved were captured and forced to denounce their name, culture, religion and, ultimately, their identity (Hall, 2009). This act of dehumanization was designed to annihilate the self, distort the imago Dei, and reinforce the idea that Black people could never be human beings because they do not look like White folk. Furthermore, dehumanization was an ideological means of crucifying Africans while keeping them alive as disposable units of labour (Hall, 2009). Existential crucifixion further describes the destruction of life that prevented the enslaved and their offspring from ever self-actualizing.

Given the lingering torture of African peoples in the Americas for over 350 years, it is impossible to fully estimate the damaging and enduring legacy of such treatment. Anne Bailey makes special reference to children and offers a vital insight when she asserts:

from what we know from the field of psychology about the importance of the formative years in shaping the future adult, again, we may only imagine the trauma of witnessing the constancy of death, dying, and violence without the palliative of traditional customs passed on by family and loved ones. Again, where the physical and psychological horrors coincided, this must have dealt additional blows to African customs, values, and psyche. (Bailey, 2007)

Reflecting on this human tragedy, or the 'Black Holocaust' as conceptualized by Joe Feagin (2000), the question is asked, how have they survived? Na'im Akbar (2001) asserts that the continued survival of Black humanity, despite these conditions, is a phenomenon of greater significance than the conditions that continually threaten Black life.

Resilience in the face of elimination – an effect of an African Caribbean heritage

Despite the continual onslaught on Black life, there are two indomitable dimensions of African Caribbean heritage that have withstood the ravages of dehumanization; first, inner strength, the life force or resilience of the African spirit; and second, a belief in the creator. The belief in the creator and its enduring legacy for people of African descent will be examined later; for now, however, we shall look at the notion of resilience.

What is resilience? On the surface, it is the ability to endure difficult times or the ability to withstand pressure; however, there is an additional component to resilience. John W. Reich et al. define resilience as an outcome of successful adaptation to adversity. For Reich and his co-authors, resilience goes beyond coping. They suggest that two important questions must be asked. First, is recovery how well people bounce back, and second, what capacity exists for moving forward after recovery? There are some difficulties with Reich's understanding of recovery. What or who defines the notion of recovery? Reich asserts, 'In traumatic episodes, people are able to decide what matters to them' (2010, p. 441).

Within African cosmology, resilience is understood as a life force, an energy that defines existence (Parham, 2002). Drawing on the laws on the conservation of energy, Parham uses an African understanding of the human spirit in which an integral dimension of spirit is found in all things living. He continues that what may be manifested in each person is a recreation of an 'old soul' whose spirit is destined to confront the challenges, pitfalls and opportunities of this lifetime (p. 40).

Enslavement did much to crush the lives of African human beings but what made endurance possible was the notion of resilience and the endurability of the African spirit. The notion of the spirit in the Western mind can be an ephemeral entity, but Parham emphasizes that the concept of the spirit 'is not some religious vision or some mystical "hocus pocus". It is the life force or energy that is fundamental to every living thing that exists in the universe' (2002).

The emphasis on the spirit being the life force found in all things connects to the belief in the creator who is the father of all and whose spirit, or essence, lives in all things. The belief in a creator leads into the final section on how religion, as a life-giving force, was used by African Caribbean people as a means of survival, recovery and advancement.

For people of African descent, a belief in the creator is not an appendage but an inseparable dimension of humanity. Such belief does not necessarily mean an adherence to religious or church affiliation, but rather the consciousness of God permeating daily existence. John Mbiti (1990) refers to 'everyone', including Africans, as a 'religious carrier', and African Caribbean people are no different. Reflecting on the 'religiousness' of African Caribbean people, Clifford Hill (1958), a former clergyperson, comments that of the migrants who arrived in Britain, '95% were regular churchgoers when back in the Caribbean'.

The African Caribbean people's religiosity came into play when faced with rejection. Their response was to retreat to a place where their faith sustained them. The religiousness of African Caribbean people is a West African cultural retention and had already been an indispensable mainstay for their ancestors on the plantations. Leonard Barrett (1975) makes it clear that slavery was 'fought not only physically but spiritually'. The arrival of European missionaries and the subsequent conversion to Christianity of many of the enslaved developed a fusion of African Traditional Religion and Christianity (Stewart,

2005). This religious mix is not without controversy as it is commonly accepted that the Christian Church was complicit in the development and maintenance of slavery (John, 1976). A belief in God, enabling their ancestors to fight enslavement both physically and spiritually, once again became a source of strength for African Caribbean people in Britain. John Mbiti (1990) demonstrates that religion permeated every dimension of African life, and modern scholarship corroborates Mbiti's argument about the inseparability of religion and life (Gehman, 2005). Thus Africans were religious before the arrival of Christianity, and while there is good ground to comment that Christianity was used to enslave people, it is also true that Christianity was used as a tool for the liberation of the enslaved (The Gleaner, 1995). Religion, therefore, was, and still is, a pivotal dimension of African Caribbean life in Britain and it is not likely that they will be jettisoning that dimension of their existence any time soon.

Conclusion

The effect of an African Caribbean heritage has yet to be fully explored. From this chapter it is obvious that an understanding of Caribbean history and its effects must be seriously acknowledged in the development of new psychological methods of care. To take such matters sincerely means a re-examination of Eurocentric theories of human psychology and an honest recognition that such constructs are not universally applicable. One wonders how courageous Western clinicians will fare in critiquing their current tools of diagnosis, because this will invariably mean that White hegemonic practices will be placed under the spotlight and the implicit reins of power, White privilege, dominance, assumed universality and control relinquished or at least loosened. Thus, administering appropriate care to a people perceived as problematic is multi-layered, involving relevant diagnoses based on an understanding of the legacy of an African Caribbean heritage and critical analysis of Whiteness.

Questions for further reflection

1 In considering the issue of race, what is it like being White? If you are not White, what is it like being you in terms of how you identify yourself in terms of colour?

2 Let us not kid ourselves, how do you deal with your prejudices, opinions and stereotypes of people who do not look like you?

3 Not seeing colour is a way of not dealing with the obvious. Using Johari's model from this chapter as a way of reflection, what is contained within the hidden areas or blindspot of your life that might get in the way of dealing with the other?

Bibliography

Akbar, N. (1996), *Breaking the Chains of Psychological Slavery*, Tallahassee, FL: Mind Productions and Associates, Inc.

Akbar, N. (2001), *Visions for Black Men*, Tallahassee, FL: Mind Production and Associates, Inc.

Bailey, A. (2007), *African Voices of the Atlantic Slave Trade: Beyond the Silence and Shame*, Kingston: Ian Randle Publishers.

Banton, M. (1953), 'Recent Migration from West Africa and the West Indies to the United Kingdom', in F. Bovenkerk (ed.), *The Sociology of Return Migration: A Bibliographic Essay*, The Hague: Martinus Nijhoff, 1974.

Barrett, L. (1975), *Soul Force: African Heritage in Afro-American Religion*, New York: Anchor Press, Doubleday.

Beckford, R. (1998), *Jesus is Dread: Black Theology and Black Culture in Britain*, London: Darton, Longman & Todd.

Clarke, H. J. (1998), *A Great and Mighty Walk*, DVD, Chicago: African Images.

Cosgrove, C. (1988), *The Cross and the Spirit: A Study in the Argument and Theology of Galatians*, Macon, GA; Mercer University Press.

Dick, D. (2009), *The Cross and the Machete: Native Baptists of Jamaica – Identity, Ministry and Legacy*, Kingston: Ian Randle Publishers.

Equiano, O. (2009), *Olaudah Equiano: The Interesting Narratives and Other Writings*, revised edn, London: Penguin Books.

Feagin, J. (2000), *Racist America: Roots, Current Realities, and Future Reparation*, New York: Routledge.

Fletchman Smith, B. (2000), *Mental Slavery: Psychoanalytical Studies of Caribbean People*, London: Karnac Books.

Garvey, M., http://www.brainyquote.com/quotes/quotes/m/marcusgarv 365148.html (accessed 29.6.2021).

Gehman, R. J. (2005), *African Traditional Religion in Biblical Perspective*, Nairobi: East Africa Educational Publishers Limited.

Gomez, M. (2005), *Reversing the Sail of the African Diaspora: New Approaches to African History*, New York: Cambridge University Press.

Graham, Brian J. and Howard, P. (2008), 'Heritage and Identity', in Brian J. Graham and Peter Howard (eds), *The Ashgate Research Companion to Heritage and Identity*, Farnham, Hants: Ashgate Publishing Limited.

Grant, P. I. (2007), *Blue Skies for Afrikans: Life and Death Choices for Afrikan Liberation*, Nottingham: Navig8or Press.

Hall, D. (2009), 'The Middle Passage as Existential Crucifixion', *Black Theology: An International Journal*, 7(1), pp. 45–63.

Hill, C. (1958), *Black and White in Harmony: The Drama of West Indians in the Big City from a London Minister's Notebook*, London: Hodder and Stoughton.

Howard, P. (2003), *Heritage: Management, Interpretation, Identity*, New York: Continuum.

James, W. (2020), *Holding Aloft the Banner of Ethiopia: Caribbean Radicalism in Early-Twentieth Century America*, London: Verso.

John, G. (1976), *The New Black Presence in Britain: A Christian Scrutiny*, London: Community and Race Relations Unit of the British Council of Churches.

Lago, C. and Thompson, J. (1996), *Race, Culture and Counselling*, Buckingham: Open University.

Leech, K. (2006), *Soul in the City: Urban Ministry and Theology*, University of Manchester: The Samuel Ferguson Lecture, 19 October 2006.

Mann, R. (2009), *Evolving Family Structures, Roles and Relationships in Light of Ethnic and Social Change*, Oxford: Oxford University Press.

Mbiti, J. (1990), *Introduction to African Religion*, Nairobi: East Africa Educational Publishers Limited.

Parham, T. A. (2002), 'Understanding Personality and How to Measure It', in Thomas A. Parham (ed.), *Counselling Persons of African Descent: Raising the Bar of Practitioner Competence*, London: Sage Publications.

Patterson, O. (1969), *The Sociology of Slavery: An Analysis of the Origins, Development and Structure of Negro Slave Society in Jamaica*, Vancouver: Fairleigh Dickinson University Press.

Pinn, A. (2003), *Terror and Triumph: The Nature of Black Religion*, Minneapolis, MN: Augsburg Fortress.

Reddie, A. (2006), *Dramatizing Theologies: A Participative Approach to Black God-Talk*, London: Equinox.

Reich, J. W., Zautra, A., Hall, J. S and Murray, K. E. (2010), 'Resilience: A New Definition of Health for People and Communities', in John W. Reich, Alex Zautra and John Stuart Hall (eds), *Handbook of Adult Resilience*, New York: Guildford Press.

Rousseau, G. S. and Porter, R. (1990), *Exoticism in the Enlightenment*, Manchester: Manchester University Press.

Silverman, H. and Fairchild Ruggles, D. (2007), 'Cultural Heritage and Human Rights', in Helaine Silverman and D. Fairchild Ruggles (eds), *Cultural Heritage and Human Rights*, New York: Springer Science and Business + Business Media.

Stewart, D. (2005). *Three Eyes for the Journey: African Dimensions of the Jamaican Religious Experience*, Oxford: Oxford University Press.

The Gleaner (1995), *Geography and History of Jamaica*, Kingston: The Gleaner Company Limited.

West, C. (2002), *Prophesy Deliverance: An Afro-American Revolutionary Christianity*, Louisville, KY: Westminster John Knox Press.

Notes

1 Conversation with my mother-in-law, a migrant of the Windrush epoch – 26 August 2010.

2 Personal conversation, University of Birmingham, UK, 2003.

3 This is still generally the case, but at the time of writing there is an international recession which is causing many young people to remain at home until the economic climate changes.

2

The Middle Passage as Existential Crucifixion

Introduction

'I don't get it.' These are the words my wife read in one of my twin daughter's schoolbooks many years ago as she struggled to understand a particular lesson. I have found myself uttering similar words as I attempt to understand the tragedy of the transatlantic slave trade. I understand the need for labour, but I am unable to comprehend the need for the level of brutality used on the lives of the enslaved Africans.

Continuing from the previous chapter, I want to explore how African people ended up arriving in the USA, the Caribbean and then the UK. I will do so by starting a conversation between the Middle Passage and the Crucifixion. The uncertain nature of theodicy raises questions regarding God's justice, suffering and the treatment of people created in the image of God. The subject of theodicy is therefore problematic. Professor of religion Anthony Pinn, in *Why, Lord? Suffering and Evil in Black Theology* (1999) articulates the complexity of the subject and questions the uncertain nature of the term as a proper category of investigation. Given the fact of the Middle Passage, how are we meant to understand it? I understand the Middle Passage as falling into four categories: Good Friday, Holy Saturday, the Resurrection, and the scars evidencing the Good Friday event. An additional section will conceptualize how the Middle Passage is played out in twenty-first-century postcolonial Britain. For a discussion on postcolonialism, R. S. Sugirtharajah offers further insights in *The Bible and the Third World: Precolonial, Colonial and Postcolonial Encounters* (2001, pp. 244–7).

The Good Friday of the Middle Passage

Good Friday concerns itself with Jesus, an innocent man crucified on a cross. This redemptive act was for spiritual prosperity
and human liberation. Crucifixion was a violent, bloody death,
and at its worst, Jesus uttered, 'My God, my God, why hast
thou forsaken me?' (Matthew 27.46). More could be said
about the Crucifixion, but how can the Good Friday motif be
used to interpret the experience of enslaved Africans?

At this point it might be helpful to define existentialism. C.
Stephen Evans (1984) argues that it is difficult to define existentialism because in a far deeper way any definition is untrue.
Existentialism asks two questions. First, does life have meaning? Second, is despair the only option left for humanity in a
sea of meaninglessness? Existentialism deals with the choices
that people make and throughout this chapter there are two
themes implicitly encoded in the literature. Question one concerns itself with the horrors of enslavement and the meaning of
life. The second question examines hope amidst despair as the
enslaved made decisions determining their future.

A metaphorical form of death began in the minds of the
enslavers prior to their arrival in Africa. A living death for the
enslaved occurred from the moment of capture and endured
throughout enslavement. One aspect of this crucifixion was
the manner of incarceration in the barracoons[1] (Pinn, 2003).
Existential crucifixion continued as the enslaved were enforced
to denounce their name, culture and, ultimately, their identity.
This act of dehumanization was an attempt to annihilate the
self, distort the imago Dei, and reinforce the idea that Black
people could never be human beings because they did not look
like White folk. Furthermore, dehumanization was an ideological means of crucifying enslaved Africans while keeping
them alive, just enough, to become profit-making units for the
development of Britain (Williams, 1964). The Good Friday of
the Middle Passage was the crucifixion of the innocent for the
benefit of the industrialization of Britain, which in turn became
the foundation of capitalism, developing market forces and,
ultimately, globalization.

The Good Friday of the Middle Passage continued as many of the enslaved died en route to the Americas. Those who became sickly through disease and a proliferation of inhuman conditions were thrown overboard as they were deemed unprofitable for the slave trader. Once disposed of, the enslavers could claim for loss of property. Despite the brutality exerted on the lives of Black people, Olaudah Equiano, a freed slave, commented on the environment of violence for both his fellow countrymen and the White crew (Equiano, 2009). Despite the gore of the Middle Passage an alternative account exists. Kamau Brathwaite (1981) suggests that the Middle Passage was misunderstood and was more than 'merely' a traumatic destructive experience that led to Africans being separated from their homelands, history and traditions. He recognizes the Middle Passage as a channel, or pathway, between the old tradition and what was being developed in the Caribbean. Brathwaite's claims must be regarded with caution. The arrival of Africans in the Caribbean was not for transporting their culture, skills, wisdom or knowledge, but as free labour for the development of the West.

Due to the Middle Passage, many Africans who had come from sophisticated civilizations spanning centuries became food for marine life in the Atlantic Ocean by way of overboard disposal, suicide, or burial in the silt of the ocean seabed. If they did not physically die, they metaphorically died living in humiliating degradation on board the slave ships. Sanitary conditions taken seriously at home did not exist in ship holds (Equiano, 2009). Unsanitary conditions and lack of oxygen below decks meant that the enslaved were forced to live in their own vomit, excreta and urine while breathing in the foul air of such living conditions (Falconbridge, 2015, p. 25). When they were let out of the holds, it was for 'exercise' and 'force feeding' (Pinn, 2003, p. 31). Exercise and forced feeding were a form of punishment. Barbara Bush, a lecturer in political studies, cites other forms of punishment, such as failing to dance and sing when compelled to do so. She continues that when the enslaved sang, their songs were 'melancholy lamentations', undoubtedly expressing the death pain of their existence (Bush, 1990).

The more enlightened enslavers employed ships' doctors who provided some form of medical care, records and hygiene checks.[2] The employment of ships' surgeons, one can only guess, was more for protecting the profits of the enslavers than being concerned for the wellbeing of the enslaved (Bush, 1990, p. 56).

Prior to disembarking in the Americas, those who survived endured the further humiliation of presale preparation. This consisted of their bodies being cleaned and oiled, and specially made bungs being placed in their anus to prevent the seeping out of the bloody flux that would have reduced the possibility of a good price for them (Walvin, 2001). No one escaped the physical or psychological horrors of the journey either as victim or witness.

It must always be kept in mind that the enslaved Africans did not hear of employment opportunities in other lands and make applications to migrate. The enslaved, being wrenched from their habitat, had an alien cosmology forced on them, with acts of cruelty and violence used to maintain the slave system and as a form of social control (Walvin, 2000).

In describing the suffering, Dianne Stewart, professor of religion, makes reference to the undeserved agony and crucifixion of Jesus. The experience of unjust suffering, persecution and death was chronic, visceral and immediate within the daily experience of the enslaved population. Some of the corporal persecution inflicted on the bondsmen and women were cruder forms of crucifixion than that of Jesus (Stewart, 2005).

Orlando Patterson, a sociologist, contends that due to the event of enslavement, our ancestors experienced a form of death. Patterson asks a poignant question. 'If the enslaved no longer belonged to a community, if they had no social existence outside of their master, then what was he [sic]?' Patterson's response was to define the enslaved as 'socially dead' (Patterson, 1967, p. 38).

The transatlantic slave trade was an event in which the black body was the receptacle for the unholy projections of the White psyche. An initial psychological interpretation of this behaviour may conclude that a mind capable of such levels of repetitive violence may reflect significant psychological disturbance. Such an investigation, in the light of modern psychological theory, may prove fruitful in trying to understand a psyche capable of carrying out such repetitive protracted treatment of innocent people and to talk of such behaviour as a product of greed is too simplistic. This chapter, however, is not an attempt to understand the psychological nature of the slave traders and slave masters.

Anthony Pinn, a Black humanist, in *Terror and Triumph* traces the development of racism, a by-product of the slave trade, and concludes that its formulation was a conglomerate of literature, foreign travel and trade, biblical misinterpretation and a normative definition of aesthetics leading to the problematizing of African bodies (Pinn, 2003).

The violence of Good Friday was played out on the humanity of the enslaved, but it must be understood more widely than physical abuse. It was about severance from the sources that gave Africans their identity, separating them from meaningful relationships, and leaving them in a state of helplessness and powerlessness and at the mercy of their enslavers.

Existential crucifixion was an experience of dehumanization that caused the enslaved Africans to taste various forms of death, but as Eric Williams, Smithsonian Curator, commented, 'they did not die'.[3]

The Holy Saturday of the Middle Passage

What occurred between the Crucifixion and the Resurrection? What are we to make of the apparent silence between life and death? Christians believe that Jesus was God, indivisible and inseparable, yet the Easter story poses problems for many people. How can God be dead? How can we conceptualize such a theological profundity? There is awkwardness in saying that God died. This paradox is articulated by Winston Persaud, Professor of Systematic Theology, when he writes 'we are talking about the God who is both present with and is, simultaneously, the crucified Christ. God is the One who suffers for the healing of humanity and for the whole creation' (Persaud, 1991, p. 127).

Alan Lewis, professor of constructive and modern theology (2001), states that Holy Saturday is omitted in many Christian settings. Something must have occurred, but what? The Bible is relatively silent on the matter, except for a few verses that allude to Jesus being in hell (see, for example, Psalm 16.10, and 1 Peter 3.19). While the disciples and others were mourning the loss of their loved one, Jesus was in hell bringing freedom to those who died believing. This view is commonly held by many Pentecostals, but not by some biblical scholars, who consider that there is little biblical or Jewish literature that regards this place as hell. How then do we understand the term 'hell'?

One understanding of hell is that it is a place where God is not.[4] That is, a place of untold torment and misery but not located on earth. Lewis, however, refers to hell as the fathomless depths of suffering which Christ endured on the cross and in his death. Lewis extends the idea of suffering to Jesus being seen as the victim of divine judgement who sank into an abyss of evil and horror to the point of separation from God (Lewis, 2001). This seems to contradict the biblical text where Paul asks the question in Romans 8.39, 'What shall separate us from the love of God?' Yet there is an apparent separation from God during Holy Saturday. So is separation, or the absence of God, possible? While this chapter does not explore separation/absence from God, this possibility exists if we conclude that Jesus, being God, died on the cross. The Easter absurdity of either the death or the separation of the creator provokes us to ask: where was God in the horrors of the Middle Passage?

As Jesus' physical body was in the tomb, where was he spiritually? One may ask the same question of the enslaved. Being present in the tomb of the slave ships, where were they? What occupied their thoughts as they lay in their makeshift living coffins, existentially dead? What were their dreams or nightmares as they psychologically straddled memories of home while existing in the humiliating here and now? How did they contend with the darkness, the moans and groans of their fellow country-people, the stench of incarcerated humanity, while being chained to each other and to death? We cannot

[handwritten annotation top: Victor Frankl – Man Search for Meaning v. Slave Experience]

[handwritten annotation right margin: RESILIENCE]

be sure, but we do have some insight into their thoughts, as they plotted to overthrow the slave ships, take their own lives, kill new-born babies rather than submit them to enslavement, yet in contradiction, continued to speak their language as well as forming positive relationships while on board. Their actions give some indication of their private and collective thoughts, as they asserted their humanity and fought for freedom. At one level, there is an indescribable event of human degradation, yet, against the odds, there were also signs of human hope, the 'soul essence', a term coined by Cheryl Grills and Martin Ajei, African-centred psychologists, describing the African understanding of the mind as spirit (Grills and Ajei, 2002). The Black theologian Dwight Hopkins argues similarly that the human spirit and the breath of God resided within each one of them, vying for expression (Hopkins, 2005). Alan Lewis writes that death is given time and space to be itself, in all its coldness and helplessness. During the darkness and terror of imprisonment in the ship's hold, how was the waiting and silence understood by the enslaved? (Lewis, 2001). Silence can at times be invigorating but can also be discomforting as it makes us face the hidden monsters of our lives that we spend most of our lives avoiding. Maybe there is a reason why the Church has not spoken too much about Holy Saturday as the horror of the cross is followed by a period of despair, unknowing and uncertainty. Of the terror of the cross, the German Reformed theologian Jürgen Moltmann emphasizes in *The Crucified God* that the cross 'is not loved and cannot be loved' (Moltmann, 1995, p. 1).

Lewis articulates that we know the outcome of the Crucifixion and the Resurrection, but from the position of the Holy Saturday, a horrible place, one can only look back at the cross, the point of crucifixion, but I would contend that before the crucifixion there must have been a time when Africans enjoyed their way of life.

We cannot know the depth of anguish endured by the enslaved Africans en route to the Americas. Jesus, having escaped death, displayed physical signs of crucifixion in his hands and feet, and the Africans, while 'victorious' in surviving

[handwritten annotation bottom: VF: Survived because he knew there was something important he needed to complete... his manuscript.]

the journey of torment, carried irreparable wounds in their bodies and intrapsychic beings.

David Goatley, Baptist missionary, investigating the dilemma of the enslaved, conceptualizes the extremes of their human suffering as 'Godforsakenness' (Goatley, 1996). Goatley takes up the Holy Saturday theme when he suggests that the ideas of absence and presence are taken up in the same person of God. If Christ is dead and God is dead, what has happened to the Spirit? Moltmann, entering a complex analysis of the separation of God and Jesus, contends that on the death of the cross the Father and Son are separated (Moltmann, 1995). What bonds them together is the Holy Spirit. The thorny question of theodicy, and where is God in the suffering of people, is an age-old question.

During the Holy Saturday of the Middle Passage then, where was God? Was he there, or was he apparently silent during this time as he so often appears to be in moments of crisis in people's lives? Or was he there operating through the enslaved as they made their attempts for freedom? In African cosmology there is no separation between the material and immaterial. Thus, to imagine the absence of God is impossible, so God was present during the Middle Passage.

If we believe that God is omnipresent, we must conclude that he was there on the ships. However, this poses a problem for many. If God is omnipresent, was he there in the evil of humanity? He was not the cause of evil, but he resided in the evil on board the ships. We are left with another problem, an uncomfortable tension that cannot be explored in this chapter. If God is in all, was he in the lives of the enslavers? The final uncertainty is how, if God is omnipotent, do we account for his apparent powerlessness during such human tragedy?

Holy Saturday, then, is a moment of extreme painful human complexity, uncomfortableness and contradiction. Nevertheless, from the conundrum of the Holy Saturday of the Middle Passage, is redemption possible from this incomprehensible human tragedy? Na'im Akbar, an African American psychologist, asks the question, 'With all that we have been through why are we still here?' (Akbar, 2007).

Holy Saturday was not the destination for Jesus; neither was the Middle Passage the destination for the enslaved. Lewis refers to Holy Saturday as a horrible place because without knowing the assurance of the Resurrection the only place to look at is the past. Whatever we make of Holy Saturday and the mystery that surrounds it, the end of the process was victory in the Resurrection.

The Middle Passage: acts of resurrection

The Middle Passage was a torrid, evil and tortuous affair. Indeed, the problem of evil has been a continual question wrestled with by philosophers and theologians. Anthony Pinn, Black humanist, explores the notion of evil as follows:

> The examination of African American responses to evil began with slavery, where the religious question of human suffering first emerges for Black Americans. Brought here as chattel in the early 1600s, African Americans have faced the brutalities of dehumanization through the destruction of their culture, the ripping apart of family units, rapes, beatings, and other actions that linked the control of black bodies with the increase of plantation profits. (Pinn, 2006, pp. 13–14)

Yet those ships of despair contained signs of hope reminiscent of the sun shining through the holes in dark clouds on a dismal day. The resurrection signs of life were a refusal to voluntarily submit to enslavement. Here I define resurrection as the attempt to become autonomous in an environment of inhuman brutality leading to social and psychic death.

Referring to his body, Jesus claimed that in three days the temple would be destroyed but he had power to raise it again (John 2.18–22). African life was treated as a disposable commodity by the White enslavers, so how were the Africans going to raise themselves in an environment that placed them on a conveyor belt of annihilation?

Acts of resurrection

Acts of resurrection occurred from the moment of capture, as many attempted to escape from the hands of the enslavers. The enslaved, although incarcerated on the ships, took control of their lives through four main areas of expression: forming relationships, maintaining their original languages while developing new ones, mutinies and suicide. How might these expressions be understood?

During my psychotherapy training, I was instructed that human beings express themselves on two levels, social and psychological. If that is the case, what was it that the enslaved were expressing by their actions? First, it was various forms of protest against the horrors of enslavement. Second, it was a dual assertion of their humanity and of the imago Dei. Third, it was an assault on a Western ideology that denied the equality and dignity of Africans. Their actions must not be seen so much as rebellion, but rather, as an inalienable expression of noncompliance to enslavement.

An aspect of life that Africans knew was crucial to their wellbeing was the forming of relationships. It was through this that communities were born. During the Middle Passage, it was not the case that they had no other choice and their circumstances prevailed; it was within an African cosmology that relationships developed their sense of identity, significance and self-worth. Chigor Chike, an African Anglican minister, examined the lives of four enslaved Africans who considered that human life only had significance when it was in relationship with other human beings (Chike, 2007). The development of relationships on board the slave ships is examined by Mervyn Alleyne, professor of sociolinguistics, when he writes that the relationships formed on the ships were significant to the point that they called themselves shipmates (Alleyne, 1988). Out of such relationships came strict sexual regulations as they considered each other as family, and such relationships, where possible, continued in the slave plantations (Patterson, 1967).

The second aspect of resurrection was the complex formation of language. Over one thousand different African languages were transported across the Atlantic (Walvin, 2000). Frantz Fanon, psychiatrist and social political writer, states 'that each language suggests a different culture' (Fanon, 1991, p. 18). However, the development of a complicated African language structure and patois is not the focus of this chapter.[5] Instead, I will suggest four reasons why there was a need for a new language. First, to enable the slaves to perform the tasks set by the slave masters. Second, due to cultural and language diversity, a new tongue was essential for communication among themselves. Third, a created common language enhanced their chances for survival. Finally, a new language increased the possibility of achieving freedom.

The third aspect of resurrection was mutinies. John Blassingame, professor of history, cites 55 mutinies on slavers from 1699 to 1845, as well as passing references to over one hundred other mutinies (Blassingame, 1979).

The final act of resurrection was suicide. It seems ironic that resurrection is about life, yet Africans chose suicide as a form of self-determination. Suicide was used as a permanent weapon of protest against the slave master, his profit, and the institution of enslavement. Such endeavours by the enslaved brought about a sense of hope amidst despair.

Frantz Fanon, referring to Algeria during their time of French colonization, echoes and encapsulates the experiences of the enslaved Africans centuries before. Of the colonized, and their bid for freedom, Fanon writes:

Confronted by a world ruled by settlers, the native is always presumed guilty. But the native's guilt is never guilt which he accepts; it is rather a curse, a sort of sword of Damocles, for, in his innermost spirit, the native admits no accusation. He is overpowered but not tamed; he is treated as an inferior, but he is not convinced of his inferiority. He is patiently waiting until the settler is off guard to fly at him … he is in fact ready at a moment's notice to exchange the role of the quarry for the hunter … The native is an oppressed person whose permanent dream is to become the persecutor. (Fanon, 1990, p. 41)

The Resurrection is not without incident. It is fundamental to the Christian faith, as it speaks of Jesus' return from the dead. Amidst the crucifixion and Holy Saturday of the Middle Passage, the enslaved confronted the physical and ideological powers of their slave masters. They would under no circumstances surrender to enslavement and domination by the enslavers. The Resurrection was a single historical event, but during the Middle Passage the trinity of the Crucifixion, Holy Saturday and the Resurrection was a sophisticated, multi-layered interplay occurring simultaneously.

Jesus rose from the dead but carried the visible marks of crucifixion. The visible scars of the nails testified to his earthly skirmish (John 20.20, 25, 27). The modern-day African Caribbean diaspora have not experienced the horrors of the Middle Passage or transatlantic enslavement, but the migrants have experienced colonialism. Yet the scars of enslavement and colonialism remain, primarily in the minds of Black folk. One of the distinguishing features of the enduring legacy of oppression is one's self-perception as a mark of shame and psychological disfigurement; Na'im Akbar argues that it is a sign that we do not love ourselves (Akbar, 2007).

While the Easter story has been employed to interpret the Middle Passage, can the same narrative be used to understand the lives of the African Caribbean diaspora in Britain? This question will be explored next.

Black crucifixion in modern Britain

The Easter narrative arguably begins with the entry of Jesus into Jerusalem. It is a scene of mass celebration that would, in less than a week, turn into a violent episode, ending his life (Matthew 21.1–11). This chapter began with the crucifixion of the Middle Passage as the moment of capture of Africans for enslavement. When Caribbean migrants, by invitation, came to help Britain rebuild its infrastructure and the wealth of the country, they came as loyal British subjects, but faced rejection when they arrived (Wilkinson, 1993). Being spurned by the Mother country, who were these British subjects now? The importing and exploitation of Black life, or non-White life, to rebuild the infrastructure and wealth of a European country is an age-old phenomenon, for which the African ancestors seem to serve as modern-day templates of exploitation.

Holy Saturday in modern Britain for the African Caribbean diaspora

What meaning does Holy Saturday carry for African Caribbean people in Britain? As previously discussed, Holy Saturday was the space between the cross and the Resurrection. Lewis records that Holy Saturday was a place of suffering, a place of not knowing and a place of uncertainty (Lewis, 2001). The only place that one can look with surety is back. Lewis' comment of looking back at the cross is partly true. For the migrants, looking back was a place called home. A place of familiarity, a place of acceptance and a place where despite their difficulties they were the dominant people group, it was their Jerusalem. A serious question that must be asked is, where or what do the subsequent generations of African Caribbean offspring consider as home, given the constant exposure of identity coming from Black America with all its materialistic trappings?

Existential crucifixion has occurred to many African Caribbean people in Britain and they are presently living in oblivion in the Holy Saturday of their lives. I do not say 'total oblivion' because many have an 'inkling' that things were not right with the fear of Brexit or with the Black Lives Matter movement but feel powerless to change their situations. This 'knowing' that things are not right concurs with the Black theologian James Cone, who comments in 'The Cross and the Lynching Tree' that some people still believe that it is right for people of African descent to suffer (Cone, 2006). Within some Christian circles there is a belief that during Holy Saturday, while people mourned, Jesus was active in preaching to those who had died in faith. During the Middle Passage, Holy Saturday was a place where the enslaved lay chained in their coffins of transportation, shackled to their counterparts, but in their spirits creating schemes, plans, and strategies to assert their humanity and express their fight for freedom.

Reflecting on the Easter story, I see the bystander who offers Jesus a sponge soaked in sour wine to deaden the pain of crucifixion (Mark 15.36). Black life in general, but Caribbean life in particular, is still considered cheap in Britain. Government initiatives providing grant aid and numerous consumer durables symbolize the wetted sponge. They are offered to deaden the pain of crucifixion, but the crucifixion continues, with many African Caribbean lives considered dispensable – as the recent Windrush scandal in the UK attests. Many are existentially crucified in prisons and psychiatric institutions, excluded from schools and universities and at the bottom of social indicators. Their position in society is a place of suffering, with little or no hope of life coming from their crucified state or the Holy Saturday of their existence. Given this bleak scenario, is there a way forward, a way for liberation?

Acts of resurrection in modern Britain for African Caribbean people

What does the idea of resurrection look like for African Caribbean people in modern Britain? In this context, resurrection means Black people being able to express themselves as human beings, and treated with equity and dignity by the host population. While in a Christian neo-conservative view, liberation means freedom from sin, Black liberation needs to be understood in a wider perspective. James Cone understands human liberation as God's work of salvation in Jesus Christ; its source and meaning cannot be separated from christological sources (Scripture, tradition, and social existence) and content (Cone, 2003). From the context of enslavement, colonialism and oppression, liberation includes freedom from all the forces that reduce an individual, or groups of people, to a non-entity or non-beings (Beckford, 2000). Liberation also means that you can pursue the possibility of achieving your potential.

While in Britain we no longer live under the brutality of the transatlantic slave trade, or the tyranny of colonialism, African Caribbean people are still a marginalized group of people. The only organization they possess, with limited autonomy, is Black Majority churches. By 'limited autonomy' I mean that many Black Majority churches have their headquarters in America and are restricted in how they manage their affairs in the UK; they are governed in how Scripture is interpreted, and headed up by White men. While it can be argued there is a need for accountability, it can also be a form of control.

Acts, or voices of resurrection, include people who speak up for oppressed groups. The earlier voices of resurrection are Valentina Alexander (1996), Robert Beckford (1998), Anthony Reddie (1998), Michael Jagessar and Anthony Reddie (2007), Mukti Barton (2005) and Emmanuel Lartey (1997).

There are two other locations that act as points of resurrection on the British landscape. First, although now to a lesser degree, there are Rastafarians. According to Robert Beckford, cultural and media critic, the Rastafarians offered an early resource for critical theological reflection on life in Britain for Black people (Beckford, 1999). The thought of Rastafarians offering a theological critique is not taken seriously by Black Majority churches, possibly due to the historical links with Marcus Garvey and to the churches in Britain being largely reticent about issues of race and injustice. The other organization that advocates Black liberation is the Nation of Islam. While it is not a Christian organization, one of its aims is the liberation of Black life in Britain, and again, like the Rastafarians, this group is generally not taken seriously.

Future trajectories for African Caribbean people in Britain

The resurrection or hope of African Caribbean people begins not with a greater accessibility to consumer durables and money but rather in the liberation of their minds. Chancellor Williams, in *The Destruction of Black Civilization* (1987), advocates that liberation must begin in the minds of our people. Furthermore, argues Williams, the liberation of the mind concerns itself with separation from the values and ideologies of the dominant group, which they use to oppress and that Black people have internalized. Williams advocates an eight-stage plan that people of African descent would have to employ to begin the process of unburdening ourselves (Williams, 1987).

While the Black Majority Church has been influential for its constituents in the 1960s and 1970s and beyond (for example, Black Boys Can, a social enterprise originating in and facilitated by the Church of God of Prophecy, aimed at developing the potential of African Caribbean boys (Excell3, 1999)), I echo the claims made by James Cone when he was asked a question about liberation and the role of the Black Church in America, following an enlightening and thought-provoking lecture on *The Cross and the Lynching Tree* (Cone, 2006). Cone articulated that the Black Church in America has lost its way. The Church focuses too much on itself to the exclusion of others. The same argument could be levelled at the BMC today. The major difference is that in America the Black Church will say that it is Black and is not ashamed to say so. In England, the BMC in general, and the Black British Pentecostal Church in particular, seldom engage with issues on race. They will not admit they are Black; neither will they engage in matters on race, politics and other related issues, because Christ has dealt with the question of race at the cross. The BMC is years behind America.

However, there is a sign of hope from the shores of Britain from the pens of Anthony Reddie, Robert Beckford and to a lesser degree Joseph Aldred who have written about the current situation of Black people in the UK. Given the horrors and violence of the Middle Passage, Emmanuel Lartey, reflecting on Stephen Lawrence, a Black British teenager murdered in 1993 in a violent racially-motivated attack, wrote persuasively in 'After Stephen Lawrence' arguing for a Black British theology highlighting ten categories requiring important reflection. Briefly, his treatise begins with creation, that every human being is created in the image of God. Second, Black theology in Britain is contextual. Third, Black theologians in Britain must use everything at their disposal to 'understand, interpret, articulate and manifest their faith'. Fourth, Black theologians in Britain derive their value from African, Caribbean and Asian roots. Fifth, Black theologians in Britain must 'embrace plurality, inter-faith interaction and dialogue'. Sixth, 'matters of enduring relevance' must be thoroughly examined, as in all theological work. Seventh, Black theologians must work with men, women and children and all are important on this huge project if they share the same goals and vision. Eighth, Black theology in Britain must be a liberative praxis. Ninth, Black theologians must work with other theologians and their work must be interdisciplinary. Finally, Black theologians must be creative in their approach and not imitate White Western liberal methods (Lartey, 1999). There is more.

Lartey pushes the remit of a Black British theology by adding another seven imperatives. It must be biblical, historical, philosophically and culturally orientated, socio-economically driven, political, psychological and aesthetic (Lartey, 1999).

In the author's mind Black theology is pastoral theology because it takes into consideration the care and cure of souls in the widest context of existence.

Conclusion

To sum up, the Middle Passage was a 400-year travesty that brutalized millions of enslaved Africans. Since then, descendants of the African Caribbean diaspora have lived their lives within a matrix of intergenerational trauma, the Crucifixion, Holy Saturday and the Resurrection. The crucifixion of our being has left an existential wound that will be with us for a long time yet.

The fate of African Caribbean people in Britain in terms of liberation enabling them to reach their potential rests on the shoulders of three main sources. First, voices of resurrection, where people who write, critiquing society, sound a warning to descendants of the African Caribbean diaspora. Second, the

BMC must not be so insular, they must intentionally extend the teachings of Jesus beyond the safety of the four walls of church, and must embody the mandate that Jesus gives, 'look up and see that the fields are white and ready for harvesting' (John 4.35). While this is often understood as people becoming Christians, another view may understand it to mean that people within the Black Church community need to take their eyes off themselves, reach out and empower the lives of others. Finally, the Nation of Islam seems at present to have a strong commitment to winning Black people to the cause. However, with all its attempts at good works it does not fit the Christian paradigm. African Caribbean lives have been crucified and, like our ancestors, there must always remain the spirit of hope and resurrection if they are ever to experience liberation as human beings and as people created in the image of God.

Questions for further reflection

1 What are your thoughts on understanding the horror of the Middle Passage?
2 What other tragedies in life might you consider a form of existential crucifixion, and why?
3 Why do you think many Christians and others in modern Western society quickly jump from the Crucifixion to the Resurrection with little or no thought to Holy Saturday? Do you have any current examples to support your answers?

Bibliography

Akbar, Na'im (2007), 'The Precedent of Repair for Reparation: The Challenge of Black Mental Health', lecture given at the 'So We May Talk before We Can Walk' Conference held at The Botanical Gardens, Birmingham, UK, 14 May 2007.

Alexander, V. (1996), 'Breaking every fetter?: To what extent has the Black-led church in Britain developed a theology of liberation?' Unpublished thesis, University of Warwick.

Alleyne, M. (1988), *Roots of Jamaican Culture*, London: Pluto Press.

Barton, M. (2005), *Rejection, Resistance and Resurrection: Speaking out on Racism in the Church*, London: Darton, Longman & Todd.

Beckford, R. (1998), *Jesus is Dread: Black Theology and Black Culture in Britain*, London: Darton, Longman & Todd.

Beckford, R. (2000), *Dread and Pentecostal: A Black Political Theology for the Black Church in Britain*, London: SPCK.

Blassingame, J. (1979), *The Slave Community: Plantation life in the Antebellum South*, Oxford: Oxford University Press.

Brathwaite, K. (1981), *Folk Cultures of Slaves in Jamaica*, London: New Beacon Books.

Bush, B. (1990), *Slave Women in Caribbean Society 1650–1838*, London: James Currey.

Chike, C. (2007), *Voices from Slavery: The Life and Beliefs of African Slaves in Britain*, Milton Keynes: Author House.

Cone, J. (2003), *God of the Oppressed*, New York: Orbis Books.

Cone. J. (2006), 'The Cross and the Lynching Tree', lecture given at Harvard Divinity School, 19 October 2006; the lecture can be seen on http://www.hds.harvard.edu/news/events_online/ingersoll_2006.html (accessed 30.9.2021).

Equiano, O. (2009), *Olaudah Equiano: The Interesting Narrative and Other Writings*, London: Penguin Books.

Evans, S. C. (1984), *Existentialism: The Philosophy of Despair and the Quest for Hope*, Grand Rapids, MI: Zondervan Publishing House.

Excell3 (1999), Black Boys Can, http://www.fbrn.org.uk/project%20 profiles/black-boys-can (accessed 30.6.2021).

Falconbridge, A. (2015), *An Account of the Slave Trade on the Coast of Africa, 1788*, Australia: Leopold Classic Library.

Fanon, F. (1990), *The Wretched of the Earth*, London: Penguin Books.

Fanon, F. (1991), *Black Skins White Masks*, London: Pluto Press.

Goatley, D. (1996), *Were You There? Godforsakenness in Slave Religion*, New York: Orbis Books.

Grills, C. and Ajei, M. (2002), 'African-Centred Conceptualisations of the Self and Consciousness: the Akan Model', in Thomas A. Parham, *Counselling Persons of African Descent: Raising the Bar of Practitioner Competence*, London: Sage Publications.

Hopkins, D. (2005), *Being Human: Race, Culture, and Religion*, Minneapolis: Fortress Press.

Jagessar, M. and Reddie, A. (eds) (2007), *Postcolonial Black British Theology: New Textures and Themes*, Peterborough: Epworth Press.

Jagessar, M. and Reddie, A. (2007), *Black Theology in Britain: A Reader*, London: Equinox.

Lartey, E. (1997), *In Living Colour: An Intercultural Approach to Pastoral Care and Counselling*, London: Jessica Kingsley Publishers.

Lartey, E. (1999), 'After Stephen Lawrence: Characteristics and Agenda for a Black Theology in Britain', *Black Theology in Britain: A Journal of Contextual Practice*, 3, pp. 79–91.

Lewis, A. (2001), *Between Cross and Resurrection: A Theology of Holy Saturday*, Grand Rapids: Wm. B. Eerdmans.

Moltmann, J. (1995), *The Crucified God: The Cross of Christ as the Foundation and Criticism of Christian Theology*, London: SCM Press.

Patterson, O. (1967), *Slavery and Social Death: A Comparative Study*, Cambridge, MA: Harvard University Press.

Persaud, W. (1991), *The Theology of the Cross and Marx's Anthropology: A view from the Caribbean*, New York: Peter Lang.

Pinn, A. (2003), *Terror and Triumph: The Nature of Black Religion*, Minneapolis: Fortress Press.

Pinn, A. (1999), *Why, Lord? Suffering and Evil in Black Theology*, New York: Continuum.

Ransford, O. (1971), *The Slave Trade: The Story of Transatlantic Slavery*, London: John Murray, Readers Union Ltd.

Reddie, A. (1998), *Growing into Hope: Christian Education in Multi-ethnic Churches*, Peterborough: Methodist Publishing House.

Stewart, D. (2005), *Three Eyes for the Journey: African Dimensions of the Jamaican Religious Experience*, Oxford: Oxford University Press.

Sugirtharajah, R. S. (2001), *The Bible and the Third World: Precolonial, Colonial and Postcolonial Encounters*, Cambridge: Cambridge University Press.

Tomlin, C. (1999), *Black Language and Style in Sacred and Secular Contexts*, New York: Caribbean Diaspora Press.

Walvin, J. (2000), *Making the Black Atlantic: Britain and the African Diaspora*, London: Cassell.

Walvin, J. (2001), *Black Ivory: Slavery in the British Empire*, Oxford: Blackwell Publishers.

Wilkinson, J. (1993), *Church in Black and White: The Black Christian Tradition in Mainstream Churches in England: A White Response and Testimony*, Edinburgh: St Andrew Press.

Williams, C. (1987), *The Destruction of Black Civilization: Great Issues of a Race from 4500 B.C. to 2000 A.D*, Chicago, IL: Third World Press.

Williams, E. (1964), *Capitalism and Slavery*, London: Andre Deutsch Ltd.

Notes

1 Barracoons were outdoor pens similar to those used to control pigs or other animals. These storage areas held the captured slaves for weeks or months until enough were accumulated to board the ships for shipment to the Americas (Pinn, 2003, p. 30).

2 The journal entries of Alexander Falconbridge as he carried out medical inspections are recorded by James Walvin in *Black Ivory: Slavery in the British Empire* and Barbara Bush in *Slave Women in Caribbean Society 1650–1838*.

3 Telephone conversation in developing this chapter, 2008.

4 Personal conversation with C. Samuel, a friend and former church member, 2007.

5 The subject of patois is described by various scholars. James Walvin in *Making the Black Atlantic* defines patois as a language that had African roots but melded with English and other European languages to produce a hybrid that made sense to the slaves (p. 70). For a more detailed reading see pp. 65–83. Barbara Bush in *Slave Women in Caribbean Society 1650–1838* refers to patois as a language of slave identity, resistance, and abuse (pp. 56, 58, 158). Carol Tomlin in *Black Language and Style in Sacred and Secular Contexts* describes in detail the development of pidgin and Creole languages as a hybrid of African and European languages.

3

Body Broken: Eucharistic Violence and the Sam Sharpe Revolt

Introduction

Chapter 2 explored the arrival of the enslaved in different parts of the West. We will now explore the inalienable rights of Black humanity and the quest for freedom on the island and plantations of Jamaica seen through the life of Samuel Sharpe.

Terrorist, revolutionary, provocateur, insurrectionist, Moses-like and Messianic icon – these are all labels that could be attached to Baptist deacon Samuel Sharpe. However he is described, his life warrants analysis beyond socio-economic, historical or socio-political factors. In *Burning for Freedom*, Delroy Reid-Salmon has bucked the trend by offering a theological interpretation of the Sam Sharpe revolt (Reid-Salmon, 2012).

Reid-Salmon's work lays a seminal foundation requiring further theological reflection and serves as a reminder to theologians that whatever happens in life there is always a theological response. Theologians are reminded that they must be prepared to grapple with the concreteness of life. This chapter explores Sam Sharpe's life and actions through the elements of the Eucharist as an example of Christian ministry as social action within a pernicious context of violence. Before taking a theological look at his life, it would be pertinent to examine the social context in which he lived.

Social context: an environment of violence

Sam Sharpe's existence was one of extreme violence. But what is meant by violence? Violence is more complex than a physical encounter threatening the life of another. Raymond Williams argues that 'violence is often now a difficult word because its primary sense is of physical assault as in "robbery with violence", yet it is used in ways not easily defined' (Williams, 1976, p. 278). Furthermore, Williams states: 'It is a long complexity. There has been some obvious interaction between *violence and violation*, the breaking of some custom or dignity … this is a part of the complexity' (p. 279). Williams' argument for the nature of violence breaks down when attempting to understand the violence meted out during the transatlantic slave trade, as one wonders what rule or custom the enslaved violated to incur such brutality.

In developing a further understanding of violence, Walter Wink argues: 'A society with an unfair distribution of goods requires violence. Violence is the only way some can deprive others of what is justly theirs. Inequality between rich and poor can be maintained only by violence' (Wink, 1998, p. 68). The violence expressed in Jamaica against the enslaved affected the whole of their humanity and existence. Thus what can be surmised is that violence was used as a form of social control. As Garnett Roper has so eloquently argued, 'The Caribbean was first organized by the Europeans as a laboratory in an experiment in social inequality' (Roper, 2012).

Wink's analysis gives a good perspective on violence, but it fails to capture the heart of the violence demonstrated during the slave trade. Cheryl A. Kirk-Duggan expresses the nature of violence beyond the unfair distribution of goods. She writes:

Violence is that which violates, destroys, manipulates, corrupts, defiles, and robs us of dignity and true personhood. Violence is the use of thought and deed within a continuum of the physical, the philosophical, and the psychological that oppresses and robs an individual or community of their gift of freedom and the sacredness of their person. Violence is a practice of idolatry: that which defames god's created order. (Kirk-Duggan, 2002, p. 3)

Kirk-Duggan depicts violence in its gory nature and her analysis emphasizes how violence is an affront to theological anthropology, disrupting the whole of humanity. In addition, both oppressor and oppressed are dehumanized by violence. Another voice in the discourse on violence is James Cone, who highlights the problem of violence and asks, who is defining violence and on what terms? He emphasizes:

> White people derived their analysis from theological and political interests that support the status quo, whereas we must analyse them in accordance with our struggle to be free. We cannot let white rhetoric about nonviolence and Jesus distort our vision of violence committed against black people. (Cone, 2003, p. 200)

Cone emphasizes that it is the people feeling the sting of violence who are best placed to articulate their experience, and as Black people they must learn to express what violence has done to them. Cone develops the conversation around violence by reflecting on the hideous act of lynching. In *The Cross and the Lynching Tree* Cone, expressing the depth of the trauma of violence, remonstrates: 'The sufferings of Black people during slavery are too deep for words and that suffering did not end with emancipation' (Cone, 2013, p. 2). His emphasis reinforces Kirk-Duggan's argument on violence, and while he does not give a clear definition of violence as Kirk-Duggan does, his examples portray the experiential terror of violence through the act of lynching. Thus one does not necessarily need a definition to grasp the nature of violence. Cone attests:

> The lynching tree was the most horrifying symbol of white supremacy in black life. It was a shameful and painful way to die. The fear of lynching was so deep and widespread that most blacks were too scared to talk publicly about it. When they heard of a person being lynched in their vicinity, they often ran home, pulled down shades, and turned-out lights

– hoping the terror moment would pass without taking the lives of their relatives and friends. (Cone, 2013, p. 15)

The act of lynching was simultaneously an inhuman and dehumanizing way to die. Inhuman, because it was an abhorrent way for a human being to treat another, and dehumanizing, because to be a Black onlooker it evoked dread and fear in those whose skin colour matched the 'strange fruits hanging from the poplar trees' (Holiday, 1959). Cone's description, in one sense, is anaemic, but his imagery conveys how lynching was portrayed while accompanied by the inescapable and unutterable emotions that those who were witnesses must have experienced. Furthermore, Cone problematizes the notion of violence, arguing that it is a fallacy to ask the question whether one supports violence or non-violence because to vie for non-violence is to accept the 'oppressors' values' (Cone, 2003, p. 200). Cone makes it clear that in an 'unjust society no one can be non-violent'. He contends, 'you are either on the side of the oppressed attempting to work out the meaning of existence within an environment of dehumanization or you are on the side of the oppressor maintaining the status quo' (p. 200).

Using the analyses of Kirk-Duggan and Cone, Samuel Sharpe, facing, seeing, hearing, feeling and being immersed within the crucible of violence could not remain neutral in the face of such humanitarian despair. Kirk-Duggan and Cone's descriptions are invaluable in understanding the devastating impact of violence on humanity, but Sam Sharpe was planted on Jamaican soil and living in the context of violence. Delroy Reid-Salmon, in 'Faith and the Gallows: The Cost of Liberation' (2010), does not define violence as Kirk-Duggan and Cone do, but rather widens the discussion by depicting it through the condition of suffering which is a constant theme throughout his thesis. People suffer because violence has been exacted on them, and in this case violence is understood as deeper than physical assaults, but rather the deliberate denial of one's humanity. Reid-Salmon demonstrates an example of such violence in Sam Sharpe's life by stating that 'The lack of information about Sam Sharpe is not because he was unimportant, but because he was not regarded as a person' (p. 154). The disregarding of another human being remains a form of violence.

To stand up against such brutality would not be without major consequences. Nevertheless, Sam Sharpe used his position of being born in the master's house to his advantage. Reid-Salmon writes, 'He worked shorter hours, less physically demanding work and was better clothed and fed' (p. 3). In this regard, he emulated in part a Moses-like figure, whose background included being trained by Pharaoh and being exposed to a lifestyle not enjoyed by his fellow Israelites. Despite his privileged lifestyle, Moses 'chose rather to suffer with the people of God than to enjoy the pleasures of sin for a season' (Hebrews 11.25). Similarly, Sharpe, through the lens of his Christian faith and his reading of the Bible, determined that slavery was not the will of God and therefore needed eliminating. As a corollary, Caribbean theologian Garnett Roper further contends that 'Sharpe was most influenced by his religious faith which was assisted by his reading strategies of the Jewish and Christian scriptures' (Roper, 2012).

Leaving the brief explanation of the horrors of violence and its impact on Black humanity, I turn now to the Eucharist and how the life of Sharpe embodied and symbolized the various stages of the sacred and mysterious meal.

The Eucharist: a model for Christian ministry and social activism

Jesus and the disciples gathered to celebrate the annual Passover, the remembrance of the deliverance from Egyptian slavery for the Children of Israel (Exodus 14). On this particular celebration of the Passover, Jesus instituted a meal that would be replicated throughout Christendom and revolutionize the gathering of Christians globally. The gathering at the table, the *churbah*, was a well-known Jewish tradition, but on this occasion the meal took an unprecedented turn. Jesus said that the bread and wine were, from this point on, to symbolize his body and blood.

Given the violent context of marginalization, oppression and slavery during the time of the Passover in the Old Testament, the early Church was born in similar circumstances under the severe hand of Roman oppression and the impending crucifixion of Jesus. However, today much of the graphic imagery of the Eucharist is seldom spoken about in reminding each participant of the context in which the meal originated. It has now become a safe, sanitized meal. The violence surrounding the broken bread/broken body and the wine representing the spilt blood of Jesus is almost lost to the imagination of those who take part in the sacrament. Thus the horror of Maundy Thursday and Good Friday is masked by a Eurocentric denial of human brutality.

Yet the Eucharist emerges within a context of deep unrest, despair and fear, and at the same time offers the promise of deliverance. In interpreting Sharpe's actions regarding the Eucharist, Dom Gregory Dix's four-stage model of the Eucharist – chosen, blessed, being broken and sharing – proves a useful tool for reflection. Dix was an English Anglican priest who focused on liturgical studies and later formulated the 'Four Action Shape of the Liturgy, namely, Offertory, Consecration, Fraction and Communion' (Dix, 2005). By using Dix's paradigm as a tool for analysis it becomes relevant to the marginalized and oppressed and speaks of social injustice and liberation.

Being chosen

A need to belong, to be significant, to feel needed and loved is an instinctive human desire. The word 'chosen', though, can evoke negative emotions from those who are negatively labelled in one way or another, and those who experience the pain of living as marginalized human beings. In other words, the idea of being chosen is problematic. The following comments serve to illustrate the thoughts with which marginalized human beings must wrestle. First, marginalized people may ask, why have I been chosen to suffer in this way? Second, if one is being chosen, what is the agenda behind the one doing the choosing? Third, if someone from the dominant group has oppressed me, what is his/her agenda in choosing me? Fourth, being in a position of marginalization reinforces the reality of the other 'not being chosen'. Fifth, being chosen can develop an air of suspicion in the one being chosen, even among one's equals.

Being chosen carries with it an 'in and out' group mentality, and for Sharpe, his life demonstrated the complexity of being chosen. On the surface of his life and that of his peers, it is hard to accept the notion of being chosen because often being chosen alludes to privilege and being recipients of special circumstances. However, James Cone suggests an alternative viewpoint. Sharpe recognized himself as a Christian and his attempt to bring liberation was an act of God. Cone emphasizes:

> If the gospel is the gospel of liberation for the oppressed, then Jesus is where the oppressed are and continues his work of liberation there. Jesus is not safely confined to the first century. He is our contemporary, proclaiming release to the captives and rebelling against all who silently accept the structures of injustice. (Cone, 1997, p. 33)

Jesus was not Cone's or Sharpe's contemporary, but his life and teachings had relevance in Sam Sharpe's life and in the lives of all those that are still oppressed today.

Sharpe was chosen from a few different vantage points. First, Cone attests that Jesus was 'rebelling against those who silently accepted the structures of injustice'. Using Cone's conceptualization, Sharpe responded against the evil structures of slavery. Furthermore, as earlier stated, Cone makes it clear that in an 'unjust society no one can be non-violent' (Cone, 2003, p. 200). You are on one side or the other. Second, from the position of his faith, Sharpe understood that he was created in the image of God, a human being and a Christian, and therefore chosen not to be passive in the face of oppression. Dwight Hopkins affirms Sharpe's actions when he quotes, 'Has God not chosen the poor in the world to be rich in faith and to be heirs of

the kingdom which he hath promised to them that love him?'
(Hopkins, 2005, p. 92). For people of the African Caribbean
diaspora, or any socially excluded group, reading the gospel
narrative shines new light on their existence because it shows
Jesus' siding with the marginalized. For example, Jesus sided
with women, lepers, the physically and mentally disabled, and
his compassion is further exemplified by his interaction with
the 'demon possessed' man in Mark Chapter 5.[1]

For dehumanized people, being chosen by God is significant
because it juxtaposes the reality of their existence. Marie-
France Becker writes, 'Jesus' incarnation remains the way
chosen by God to tell us the value we have in his eyes and
thus, to reveal to us our own grandeur' (Becker, 2009. p. 63).
This 'grandeur' is not a narcissistic, arrogant self-importance
or loftiness, but rather a sense of value, worth and mystery
as one created in the image of God. Reflecting on the life of
Sam Sharpe and the notion of being chosen brings to life, in
almost a three-dimensional manner, the image on the cover of
Burning for Freedom and the sermon preached by Elizabeth
Kaeton.[2] She proclaims:

A story is told in *The Autobiography of Ms. Jane Pitman*,
that when a child was born on the plantation, the proud
parents, within hours of its birth, would bundle the new-
born and bring the baby to Ms. Pitman's cabin. The parents
would place the baby on her lap, and Ms. Pitman would say
to the parents, 'Name this child.' When the parents spoke
the child's name for the first time, she would raise the child
toward heaven and speak the child's name to God, adding
the great African prayer, 'Behold, the only thing greater than
yourself.' Then, Ms. Pitman would cuddle the baby, whispering into the child's ear, 'Is you da one? Is you da one, chile,
who will lead our people out of the darkness of bondage into
the bright new day of freedom? Is you da one?' Although Ms.
Jane Pitman was a fictitious character, the hope expressed by
her character was quite real. Her lament for someone to find
the road to freedom for those who are held in bondage is but
an echo of an ancient cry. (Kaeton, 2001)

In Reid-Salmon's publication (2010), the artist captures in pictorial form the idea shared by Kaeton by providing a historical timeline of the images of enslavement amidst a myriad of contradicting images and emotions. First, the baby is held up in anticipation of the possible one chosen to lead the enslaved to freedom. In the foreground there are some unshackled enslaved, rejoicing in their newfound freedom, while in the murky distance slave ships still carry human cargo to toil in the Caribbean land for the production of sugar for financial gain and the advancement of Europe. Was there a Jamaican matriarchal equivalent to Kaeton's fictitious character whispering in the ear of the new-born Sharpe, 'Are you da one?' ... 'or do we look for another?' If no one whispered in his ear, it may have been simply an innate sense by Sharpe that he was chosen by God. Sharpe saw the prevailing circumstances and, motivated by his Christian faith, was compelled to address the situation of societal inequality. Being chosen and wanting to respond to felt needs can lead to a strong sense of significance.

Being blessed: a human being created in the image of God

The next stage in the Eucharist is being blessed. Here, ĕulŏgĕo is referred to by Dix as 'to speak well of, to invoke a benediction upon, to prosper'. It depends who is doing the speaking and what is taking place in the life of the person being blessed. While an inanimate object such as bread is being prayed over, being 'blessed' has a positive note; but for those living in the crucible of suffering, being considered 'blessed' is often difficult to fully comprehend.

Using the eucharistic narrative as a lens for analysis, it is challenging to ask how Sam Sharpe was blessed. In White slave master terms, Sharpe was not a blessed human; however, employing Delroy Reid-Salmon's theological lens for contemplating the Baptist War, it is clear that significance is laid upon all human beings because they are created in the image of God, and for that reason alone, they are simultaneously blessed.

From the time of his birth in 1801 Sharpe's eyes would have witnessed scenes of violence and his ears would have heard the crack of the whip and the agonies of his people being brutalized by the enslavers. Furthermore, simply to talk of sight and sound is to limit Sharpe's experience on the sugar killing fields. His encounter would have been a graphic multisensory episode of existence. No doubt there would be physical and physiological responses accompanying the sights and sounds, causing hairs to stand up on his body. The potential smell of death as he cradled the tortured bodies of the enslaved in his arms ensured that his entire body did not escape the horrors of enslavement; yet without question his people were chosen by God and blessed. Oral Thomas, theologian, indicates how Sharpe understood the idea of being blessed:

> Based on the understanding that before God and in Christ, all persons were created equal in freedom and no social distinctions existed and the natural equality meant that the White man had no authority to hold the black man in slavery, a rebellion of 'passive resistance' was hatched. (Thomas, 2010, p. 30)

The sacred book that had been used to enslaved millions of Africans became the tool of liberation as Sharpe understood that slavery was not the will of God and that all humanity was created to be free. In further support to the problematic notions of being blessed, C. L. R. James writes:

> The difficulty was that though one could trap them like animals, transport them in pens, work them alongside an ass or a horse and beat them both with the same stick, stable them and starve them, they remained, despite their Black skins and curly hair, quite invincibly human beings; with the intelligence and resentments of human beings. (James, 2001, p. 9)

James refers to the resilience of Black people who, despite the odds stacked against them, were able to endure treatment difficult to imagine, while demonstrating a level of human dignity. James captures an indistinguishable dimension of humanity, notably in this case the African personality, seen simply as objects for working to death, yet containing within them a spirit of survival and defiance.

Discussing the troubling and accepted notions of being blessed, I distance myself from the clichéd and well-worn, popularized sayings of 'too blessed to be stressed' uttered in some church circles, accompanied by the associated notion of a feel-good factor. Such terms are used indiscriminately by some lay Christians and clergy alike as if they are the magician's magic words or spell that somehow mysteriously anaesthetize the pains of reality. Such terms are a denial of reality.

Examining the life of Jesus as being blessed, through such clichéd understanding, is a far cry from the life he experienced as evidenced in Scripture. An important aspect of Jesus' life is the Incarnation. That is, God taking on human flesh with all its limitations and living among humanity. James Cone offers another perspective on the Incarnation and a focus on the Black cause and contends:

> The convergence of Jesus Christ and the black experience is the meaning of the Incarnation. Because God became human in Jesus Christ, God disclosed the divine will to be with humanity in our wretchedness. And because we blacks accept God's presence in Jesus Christ as the true definition of our humanity, blackness and divinity are dialectically bound together in one reality. (Cone, 2003, p. 33)

God enters the earth and lives among the poor and oppressed and that is the centre of Jesus' life, and as Black people look within the Scriptures, they are led to believe wholeheartedly that the Bible message includes them. Cone, however, offers more insight into the Incarnation: 'This is what the Incarnation means. God in Christ comes to the weak and the helpless, and becomes one of them, taking their condition of oppression as his own and thus transforming their slave-existence into a liberated existence' (p. 77).

Jesus clothed himself in humanity, and Christians, committed to patterning their lives on him, recognize that incarnational embodiment is not an easy option; it is one that can only be voluntarily embraced, and in doing so it makes living life all the more difficult.

Reflecting on the life of Sam Sharpe, the notion of being blessed as associated with a feel-good factor, while witnessing the abhorrent treatment of his people, could not be further from the truth. Sharpe did not sidestep the concerns of his people, but recognizing he was blessed he responded to the revealed will of God by being an active participant in the liberation of his people. Despite his external reality, there was an unshakeable conviction that he and his people were chosen and blessed by God (Reid-Salmon, 2012, p. 70). The third stage of the Eucharist leads to the brokenness of the bread, a violent action.

Being broken: fragmentation of a people

In the third phase of Dix's four-stage eucharistic model, Jesus breaks the bread with his hands. Ward Powers (2008) argues that 'the breaking of bread was thus associated with the prayer of thanksgiving and had a religious significance of joint fellowship in sharing and enjoying the blessings of God'. Yet in the context of the Last Supper this meal was eaten in the shadow of the ensuing violence of the arrest, crucifixion and death of Jesus. Resurrection would follow, but only after a life being first terminated. The words of Jesus at this gathering depict the occasion of this meal when he places huge significance on the bread after blessing it. He utters, 'This is my body which is broken for you.'

The notion of being broken is problematic for marginalized people. Who does the breaking and why are we broken? Reflecting on this concept one wonders whether it is God or circumstances that cause the breaking. Human beings bristle at the thought of being broken. We find it uncomfortable, undesirable and are highly resistant to it, but the irony is that it is often through the brokenness of life that good can emerge. That too is highly contested by many because such thoughts are deeply unsavoury, especially for people who experience life as a continual process of being broken. Yet, on various levels, life teaches us that before we are able to access the goods we have purchased, a breaking of the package or seal needs to occur. This is assumed and is considered a necessary requirement for inanimate objects, but to conceptualize the brokenness in relation to human beings is fiercely resisted.

Sam Sharpe and his people were born in a state of brokenness, a position I refer to as existential crucifixion, where one's existence is denied and shadowed by the constant threat of material and immaterial extinction (Hall, 2009, p. 48). Sharpe and his peers did not start life as equals with their slave masters and, through a series of bad choices, plummet into the enslavement abyss. No, from their first breath until their last they were often only one breath away from annihilation. Their life, characterized by having no worth or human potential, did not render them powerless to transcend the imposed degradation of their social context. Sharpe, being cognisant of his environment, took on the mantle of exercising power to act on behalf of his people. He demonstrated love for his people by a conviction for justice and liberation, and by following the example of Jesus by 'laying down his life for his friends' (John 15.13). In this setting, brokenness is seen in Sharpe's life as identifying with and being in solidarity with the enslaved. Acting in solidarity does not mean watching from the sidelines, but a full engagement with the oppressed, feeling the pain and degradation and wanting to bring about social change. The willingness to participate in suffering cannot be taken light-heartedly because suffering cannot be quantified. Robinson A. Milwood encapsulates in part the brokenness experienced by Sharpe and his peers on the sugar plantations when he writes:

> Men of anthropological inspiration such as Paul Bogle, Sam Sharpe and Cudjoe were the 'Moses' of the sugar plantation slave trade. The measure of human suffering cannot be

measured or estimated by any chronological means such as conferences, committees, delegations or political eloquence. Rather, it is measured by the sacrifice of slave men, women and children. The choice of death rather than slavery. The choice of manumission to enslavement. Human dignity rather than dehumanization. (Milwood, 2007. p. 176)

The quest for freedom was not through debate and intellectual discussion, but rather was self-sacrificial. Remaining in slavery without resisting its powerful grip was contrary to the innate human desire for freedom. In the context of plantation life, liberation was not going to be handed on a plate. It would be hard fought for. There would be no other way as people who have power are seldom interested in sharing any of it. As Reid-Salmon portrays the life of Sharpe, 'experiencing suffering and death has established a Black tradition of embodied faith based on the emancipatory purpose of Jesus Christ'. Reid-Salmon further contends that, 'Sharpe and his fellow freedom fighters gave their lives in confidence, dignity and courage in a similar manner to the prophetic description of the crucified Christ' (Reid-Salmon, 2012, p. 76).

In one sense, Sharpe's life exhibited a paradoxical existence. He was born in a broken state, yet having access to certain privileges chose to give his life as an act of liberation. In doing so he demonstrated self-determination in pursuing liberation for himself, his people and his oppressors. What appears to be a paradox in Sharpe's life, claims Reid-Salmon, is the way 'faith sees the distorted relationship between God's purpose and the human condition. Faith sees oppression, exploitation and suffering and then reads this reality differently by motivating the oppressed to act against such contradictory conditions' (p. 80). In other words, their liberation would not occur without paying a heavy price for freedom.

The breaking of bread does not end there. There is a sharing of the broken elements with other participants as demonstrated by Jesus in the eucharistic narrative. Using the bread as a symbolic motif, we next explore the question of how Samuel Sharpe shared his brokenness.

The legacy of sharing one's brokenness

In the closing moment before the disciples ate the bread, Jesus, having taken the bread, blessed it, broke it, and shared it among them. The term 'giving' has wide implications, but in this instance it is used to signify how Jesus suffered and gave his life as an example for believers to follow. On the plantation Sharpe is observed suffering with his people. From the small collection of documented evidence, Sharpe served as both a member of the Native Baptist Church and a deacon in the Baptist Church. Thus he was a servant of God to the people of God, to the church and for society. His role transcended the strictures of the four walls of the sanctuary and incorporated all those who belonged to the African diaspora in the Caribbean. Theologically speaking, he exercised an incarnational ministry. From the insights of his faith, he understood that slavery was not the will of God and he now had a God-given responsibility to share this knowledge with others.

Sharpe's multi-layered life and the various strands it crossed is complex, but within this framework it is possible that he could be seen as a 'wounded healer'. The term was coined by the depth analyst Carl Jung, who used 'the Greek legends about centaur Chiron' to describe it, 'a healer who received an incurable wound from a poisoned arrow, and about Asclepius, another healer, who was wounded and killed by a thunderbolt from Zeus for taking his healing art beyond human bounds in raising the dead'. Jung conceptualized that the 'analyst is compelled to treat their patient because they too are wounded' (Allen and Wolterstorf, 2011, p. 85).

The notion of the 'wounded healer' is developed by Henri Nouwen, a Jesuit priest, in this way:

> In the middle of our convulsive world, men and women raise their voices time and again to announce with incredible boldness that we are waiting for a Liberator. We are waiting, they announce, for a Messiah who will free us from hatred and oppression, from racism and war – a Messiah who will let peace and justice take their rightful place. (Nouwen, 1994, p. 81)

Where does this Messiah come from, one may ask, and who is this liberator? The liberator is both the 'wounded minister and the healing minister' (Nouwen, 1994, p. 82). Moreover, Nouwen, using the life of Jesus as a ministerial liberative paradigm, emphasizes the uses of one's own wounds as a source of healing. These wounds include 'alienation', 'separation', 'isolation' and 'loneliness' – feelings that would have been experienced by the enslaved (p. 82). Deeper reflection on the wounded healer is provided by Edward Wimberly. Wimberly states that in the early stages of his understanding of pastoral theology the wounded healer concept could be used if the 'village was intact' and if the wounded healer was 'supported by the community and God in healing the wounds of others'. However, he acknowledges that due to the 'village not being intact' his view has shifted to another position (Wimberly, 2010, p. 111), which I will develop later.

Wimberly's earlier position is challenged by Lee Butler, who argues that he is not in favour of the wounded healer concept because 'too many black people have over identified with the term from Isaiah 53 where the prophet declares, "Jesus was wounded for our transgressions ... and by his stripes we are healed"'. Butler writes powerfully that 'We have been wounded by the transgression of others and not for the transgression of others' (Butler, 2000, p. 125). Butler favours the more wholesome term of 'loving healers', where he emphasizes that 'grieving for our wounds have been too long' and he wants it to come to an end (p. 125). Butler cautions against a romanticized dimension of being a wounded healer. His perspective, quite rightly, comes from the position that enslaved suffering was not self-inflicted but rather a process of imposed dehumanization.

In more recent times Wimberly has moved on from his earlier understanding of the wounded healer and that of Butler. Recognizing the limitations of the wounded healer, Wimberly developed 'a paradigm shift in my thinking to the role of the Bible as caregiver or as a pastor' (Wimberly, 2010, p. 112). The Bible in the life of Sharpe served as a catalyst in mobilizing the enslaved in their quest for freedom. In addition, the village, as argued by Wimberly, was not intact and Sharpe's position of taking responsibility for his freedom demonstrated that he was not 'grieving for his wounds' and the position of enslavement must now surely come to an end.

With the Bible as 'caregiver and pastor' one could assume that the focus is now deflected from Sharpe, but this is not so. Wimberly's argument is that 'Modernity made it difficult to appropriate pre-Enlightenment approaches to practical theology' (p. 112). The significant point in Wimberly's analysis is that 'it was the faith community that formed the pastoral caregiver, and the pre-enlightenment community used doctrine and the scriptures as communal resources for care' (p. 112). The use of the Bible avoids a focus on an individual undertaking of liberation, yet the quest for liberation does not exclude the individual's story. Moreover, Wimberly posits the notion of conflict-free or anxiety-free story-telling in which the pastoral caregiver, or in this case Sam Sharpe, uses their stories, which have been sufficiently worked through to bring about healing in the lives of others (p. 113). This does not mean that Sharpe would have resolved all his hurt and pain in order to be an agency of healing in the lives of others. Sharpe, using and working through his story, helped himself and his people to move forward to a new place of liberation. In a deeper way, according to Nouwen, 'True liberation is freeing people from the bonds that have prevented them from giving their gifts to others. This is true not only for individual people but also – particularly – for certain ethnic, cultural, or marginalized groups' (Nouwen, 1994, p. 63). In sharing his life Sharpe was making a strong claim that freedom was possible in the here and now, but it costs, as will now be made clear.

Do this in remembrance of me: Sharpe's life as a motif for liberation

Following the institution of the Eucharist, the next few scenes in the Gospels gather momentum in the events leading to Jesus' death. Neither he nor the disciples remain at the table. No direct command is given, but the sound of 'come follow me, do as I have done' is silently discerned between the lines of the narrative. There was a time when Jesus told those who were following him that they would have to eat his flesh and drink his blood (John 6.41–71). This, according to John's Gospel, was met with the response of, 'This is a hard saying; who can understand it?' (John 6.60). Within moments many of those following him 'went back and walked with him no more' (John 6.66). Jesus asked his original disciples, 'Will you also go away?' (John 6.67). The bid for life, freedom, liberation and emancipation comes at a great cost, and for some the cost is too great. Sam Sharpe gathered people who were going to join hands with him in solidarity, not so much with him as a person, but committed to the bigger picture of liberation for the enslaved. As a sign of commitment and solidarity, he led the way by 'kissing the Bible' (Reid-Salmon, 2012, p. 8).

During the celebration of the Eucharist Jesus offers the following words: 'as often as you do this, do this in remembrance of me' (1 Corinthians 11.24–25). The question is, 'What are we to remember?' Too often, modern-day Christians readily remember the 'good' things we have read about Jesus. We remember the healings and miracles he performed. We remember him walking on water, but too often we fail to acknowledge the tension he caused when he challenged the hypocrisy of the religious people of the day. We fail to see his encounter with the woman at the well in John 4 as breaking the taboo of a male teacher speaking to a five-times divorced woman in public. In addition, as he spoke with her, he was confronting over seven hundred years of racism and what might seem an eternity's worth of sexism (Hennigan, 2012). It is easy to forget Jesus' actions as he confronted situations, and many have embraced a personal, self-centred theology that espouses 'As long as I am all right that is all that matters.' Sharpe's life provides an example of ministry that is not centred on self but focuses on the life of freedom for other people. His model of ministry is countercultural to much of the popularized ministry that is witnessed today, especially in the West.

Delroy Reid-Salmon, writing about the 'power of the oppressed', calls on biblical witnesses as paradigms for liberation, namely the Exodus, the Prophetic Tradition and the gospel of Jesus Christ (Reid-Salmon, 2012). All of these lay stress on acts of self-sacrifice. Reid-Salmon is right in doing so but misses a crucial element at the heart of the Christian community, the Eucharist. What must be remembered is that the Eucharist was an annual celebration of the Exodus of the Children of Israel from Egypt. The act of liberation was a gruesome affair surrounded by violence initiated by killing an innocent lamb for each household, which permitted the Angel of Death to kill all Egyptian firstborn, including animals, in homes where there was no sign of the slaughtered lamb's blood on the door frames of the houses (Exodus 14).

On reflection, the eucharistic embodiment adds importance to the weight and cost of human liberation. Considering this assertion, Tissa Balasuriya argues that 'the Eucharist is central to the Christian community and encapsulates Jesus' stance for human liberation and fulfilment' (Balasuriya, 1979, p. 1). Furthermore, Balasuriya writes, 'He courageously opposed every form of oppression and injustice. His obedience to God His Father was in this service to humanity. He wanted his followers to do likewise' (p. 1). As the Passover mobilized the Children of Israel to move out from the land of Egypt, similarly the Eucharist is a call to follow Christ in the act of liberation for all fellow human beings.

Sam Sharpe: love embodied; love demonstrated

A scrutiny of Sam Sharpe's life epitomizes a man who was not driven by anger, vengeance, hatred, retaliation, or rage. While in his prison cell he was visited by Henry Bleby, a Methodist minister, who states that Sharpe emphasized that he had not been mistreated by his slave master, and that 'His master, Sam Sharpe Esq., and his family were always very kind to him' (Bleby, 1853, p. 116). However, in his personal reflections and reading of the Bible he understood that 'the white man had no more right to hold black people in slavery, than the black people had to make white people slaves' (Bleby, 1853).

Bleby captures the melancholic undercurrent, sadness and despair of Sharpe as he 'expressed deep regret that such an extensive destruction of property and life had resulted from the conspiracy he had promoted' (Bleby, 1853). Sharpe, saddened at the loss of life and the extent of the damage, continued to claim that such devastation was never his intention. In Sharpe's quest for liberation, he had not factored in the manifestation of violence that would be meted out by the slave masters at his request for payment and their interpretation of his appeal for liberation as a threat to some of their power. As a counter response to what happened, James T. Murphy Jr states that 'What cannot be avoided is the fact that God has used violence to change conditions for the betterment of his people' (Murphy, 2012, p. 99). Yet, with his fate of execution sealed, Sharpe held onto his faith and firm conviction by uttering, 'I would rather die upon yonder gallows than to live in slavery' (Bleby, 1853).

With that said, there is one aspect of Sam Sharpe's life that has had little or no consideration by scholars. Here was a man whose faith was motivated by a love of God, a love for his people and the love of freedom for all people. The type of love he embodied was not the commercial popularist notion of love, but in line with the Eucharist he demonstrated a self-sacrificial love by how he lived in giving his life for the liberation of his people and humanity. One must bear in mind that around the eucharistic table Jesus shared his bread fully cognisant that Peter would deny him and Judas would betray him. This strange new moment that symbolized Jesus' liberative act for humanity took place in the presence of denial, betrayal and fierce and violent opposition. Considering the social environment in which Sharpe was born, and given that he served in the master's house, he could have enjoyed the 'marginal' benefits of being a house slave rather than a field slave. Yet his life demonstrated that he would 'rather suffer with his people than to enjoy the pleasure of sin for a season' (Hebrews 11.25).

Sharpe's embodied eucharistic love transcended eating the bread and drinking the wine. He sacrificially shared and gave his life for his friends. One must admit that Sharpe would have been justified in hating his oppressors for their barbaric treatment of his people. We are not privy to Sharpe's introspection or private inner musings, but as the accounts of Bleby are read, there is a sense of peace accompanying Sharpe as he sits on death row acknowledging that, despite the loss of life and the destruction of buildings, he had done nothing wrong (Bleby, 1835).

His love for freedom reached beyond his own people because he understood that with the institution of enslavement the oppressors needed liberating too. Delroy Reid-Salmon contends that Sharpe understood that 'equality was for all people and his standpoint acted as a major confrontation to white hegemony which asserted a black Christian theological anthropology' (Reid-Salmon, 2012, p. 152). He recognized that despite the enslavers accruing huge profits, morally, spiritually and existentially there were no winners. All suffered in the transatlantic slave trade as victim and oppressor because they lived an existence contradictory to the image in which they were created.

In recent times, and in many areas of the world, the word love has taken on a more general and superficial meaning. For many, the idea of love is nothing more than having good feelings when things are done for them. Not so with Sharpe. Deep within Sharpe's well of faith existed a capacity to love which he was able to draw on to transcend humanity's natural proclivity to violent retaliation when being aggrieved and exploited.

While there has been a focus in the Christian tradition within the Caribbean context on the need for healing from the ravages of the transatlantic slave trade, Emmanuel Lartey in *Postcolonializing God: New Perspectives on Pastoral and Practical Theology*, which brings to the fore Ghana's fiftieth anniversary of Independence and the two hundredth anniversary of the abolition of the North Atlantic slave trade, reminds the reader:

> On this occasion it was clear in the prayers of Christian, Muslim and Indigenous religionist that each recognized a great evil had been perpetrated against the people, and what was being sought through prayer was forgiveness, healing, and reconciliation. Each religious leader made reference in their prayers to their respective sacred texts (written and oral) in seeking divine wellbeing for all the descendants of those who had been involved in the heinous trade. (Lartey, 2015, p. 6)

The violent epoch was not only felt by Christians. All the major religious groups in Ghana recognized that injustice in inhumane proportions had been exacted on African land and African peoples and thus healing was needed for all.

Conclusion

Baptist deacon Sam Sharpe's life and actions cannot be seen in socio-economic, historical, or socio-political terms only. To exclude the ministerial dimension of his life is to compartmentalize his humanity. Upon realizing that slavery had been abolished, he confronted the violent enslaving machinery by asking to be paid for work carried out by his people. Asking for payment for work done was a confrontation and challenge, and an assertion of Black humanity in the face of the powers that be, without being violent. Merely asking for monetary exchange for labour altered the relationship between slaver and the enslaved, and as such was met with violent opposition from those who sat in the seat of power and privilege. Furthermore, by confronting the powers, Sharpe embodied the Eucharist as a lived experience of being chosen, blessed, broken and laying down his life by sharing it in his fight for human liberation and fulfilment for all. Thus, like the life of Jesus, Sharpe was not justifying or sacralizing violence. Rather, he was nullifying it (Roper, 2012). In other words, as Jesus was the ultimate sacrifice for the sinfulness of humanity, Sharpe, while not paying the same price for the whole of humanity, was attempting to put an end to the enslavement of his African brothers and sisters. To do so cost him his life, but it brought freedom for thousands of his people and helped to set in motion a global change of epic proportions. Reflecting on the cost of embodying the Eucharist, Balasuriya writes:

> To Jesus' mind, the Eucharist was essentially action orientated. It was a prayer and an offering in the midst of his public life at the height of his involvement in the political issues of the time ... For him, it was united to the fundamental option to die rather than to live in compromise. It was a calculated risk. He placed his confidence in the survival of his message and spirit even if his body were to be killed. (Balasuriya, 1979, p. 17)

Sharpe understood the seriousness of human liberation and concluded that if freedom was to become a living reality it would possibly cost him his life. Yet his act at that time was not simply an act for his time alone; his example was to transcend his time and place and become a model for ministry, social action and human liberation.

Questions for further reflection

1 Why do you think we often sanitize the eucharistic service in our practice?
2 Examining the life of Sam Sharpe, how do you think your life would have to change if you were to live as an example of the human Eucharist?

Bibliography

Allen, C. L. and Wolterstorff, N. (2011), *A Liturgy of Grief: A Pastoral Commentary on Lamentations*, Grand Rapids, MI: Baker Academic.

Balasuriya, T. (1979), *The Eucharist and Human Liberation*, London: SCM Press.

Becker, M. (2009), *15 Days of Prayer with Saint Marie Clare of Assisi*, New York: New York City Press.

Bleby, H. (1853), *Death Struggles of Slavery: Being a Narrative of Facts and Incidents, which Occurred in a British Colony, During the Two Years Immediately Preceding Negro Emancipation*, London: Hamilton, Adams and Co.

Butler, L. (2000), *A Loving Home: Spirituality, Sexuality, and Healing Black Life*, Minneapolis: Fortress Press.

Cone, J. (1997), *Black Power and Black Theology*, New York: Orbis Books.

Cone, J. (2003), *God of the Oppressed*, New York: Orbis Books.

Cone, J. (2013), *The Cross and the Lynching Tree*, New York, Orbis Books.

Dix, G. (2005), *The Shape of the Liturgy*, London: Bloomsbury T & T Clark.

Hall, D. (2009), 'The Middle Passage as Existential Crucifixion', *Black Theology: An International Journal*, 7(1), pp. 45–63.

Hennigan, B. (2012), *Are we all Equal?* https://brucehennigan.com/2012/12/03/are-we-all-equal/ (accessed 20.9.2021).

Holiday, B. (1959), 'Strange Fruit', live 1959 [Reeling in the Years Live Archive], YouTube – https://www.youtube.com/watch?v=-DGY9HvChXk (accessed 20.9.2021).

Hopkins, D. (2005), *Being Human: Race, Culture and Religion*, Minneapolis: Fortress Press.

James, C. L. R. (2001), *The Black Jacobins: Toussaint L'ouverture and the San Domingo Revolution*, London: Penguin Books.

Kaeton, E. (2001), '"Is you da one?" A Sermon for the Season of Reconciliation', The Church of the Redeemer, Morristown, NJ. http://telling-secrets.blogspot.com/2021/07/is-you-da-one.html (accessed 29.9.2021).

Kirk-Duggan, C. (2002), Introduction to *Pregnant Passion: Gender, Sex, and Violence in the Bible*, Leiden: The Society of Biblical Literature.

Lartey, E. (2015), *Postcolonializing God: New Perspectives on Pastoral and Practical Theology*, London: SCM Press.

Milwood, A. R. (2007), *European Christianity and the Atlantic Slave Trade: A Black Hermeneutical Study*, Milton Keynes: AuthorHouse.

Murphy, J. T., Jr (2012), *Defining Salvation in the Context of Black Theology*, Bloomington, IN: Xlibris Corporation.

Nouwen, H. (1994), *The Wounded Healer: Ministry in Contemporary Society*, London: Darton, Longman & Todd.

Powers, W. (2008), 'The Meaning of "the Breaking of Bread"', https://bwardpowers.blogspot.com/2008/12/meaning-of-breaking-of-bread.html (accessed 20.9.2021).

Reid-Salmon, D. (2010), 'Faith and the Gallows: The Cost of Liberation', in Anthony G. Reddie (ed.), *Black Theology. Slavery and Contemporary Christianity*, London: Taylor and Francis Group.

Reid-Salmon, D. (2012), *Burning for Freedom: A Theology of the Black Atlantic Struggle for Liberation*, Kingston: Ian Randle Publishers.

Roper, G. (2012), 'Sam Sharpe in the Context of the Struggle for Freedom and Equality in the Caribbean: Freedom, Innate Desire or Acquired Appetite', paper presented at Sam Sharpe Conference, Kingston, Jamaica, 10–12 October 2012.

Thomas, O. (2010), *Biblical Resistance Hermeneutics within a Caribbean Context*, London: Routledge.

Williams, R. (1976), *Keywords: A Vocabulary of Culture and* Society, London: Croom Helm Ltd.

Wimberly, E. (2010), *African American Pastoral Care*, revised edn, Nashville: Abingdon Press.

Wink, W. (1998), *The Powers that Be: A Theology for the Third Millennium*, New York: Doubleday.

Notes

1 Mark chapter 5. Traditionally, this story is used as an evangelistic sermon in Pentecostal services, yet when the demoniac is asked his name, he does not know who he is. Common sermonic tone would be to refer to him as being demon possessed, but could not his words mean that his confusion surrounds his identity? Similarly, for many African Caribbean people born in Britain, there is a dilemma in terms of identity. For example, if someone says they are Black British, what country is he or she from?

2 The artist who painted the Emancipation Picture.

4

Eucharistic Encounters: Towards an African Caribbean Diasporan Pastoral Theology

Healing begins where the wound was made. (Walker, 2012)

Introduction

Continuing to use the Eucharist as a lens to look through, in this chapter I explore interpersonal conflict within an African Caribbean faith community. To do so is to lay the initial groundwork for developing an African Caribbean diasporan pastoral theology for the Black Majority Church (BMC) in Britain. In this context, I make explicit reference to 'Black' referring to people of African descent who were forcibly severed from their homeland, enduring the horrors of the Middle Passage and intentional dehumanization through the institution of enslavement for more than three centuries.

Although the emphasis in this chapter is the embryonic development of a pastoral theology for the African Caribbean diaspora by using Black theology as a dialogue partner, the model can be used for all people who are marginalized, exploited or broken by life's complexities.

At the time of writing the article that is the basis of this chapter, I was an ordained Bishop in the Church of God of Prophecy, a Pentecostal denomination in the UK. I had local church responsibilities, while having the oversight of seven congregations for the Church of God of Prophecy in the North-East of England. In addition, I am a trained psychodynamic counsellor with over 25 years post-qualification experience.

Towards a pastoral theology for an African Caribbean diaspora

In developing this new paradigm, I used the pastoral cycle as described by Emmanuel Lartey (Lartey, 2003). Lartey used this cycle in gathering a group of people from widely diverse backgrounds of country, ethnicity, age and gender, with a 'Shared commitment to learning for the purpose of being reflective practitioners of pastoral care in one form or another' (p. 131). Lartey's pastoral cycle comprised five stages/phases. First, reflecting on the *'concrete experience'*. This is where the participant describes in detail the specific incident requiring exploration. It is the lived experience recorded in detail. The second phase Lartey describes as *'situational analysis'*. An alternative description is 'psychosocial exploration', where there is respectful engagement with the humanities, offering a 'multiperspectival' gaze for a clearer grasp in understanding the situation. Phase three is the *'theological analysis'*. This section questions the previous two stages through a theological lens, evoking queries such as 'What questions arise from my faith concerning what I have experienced and the analysis of it?' (p. 133). To respond to such questions much 'reading and research is required'. Phase four is 'situational analysis of theology', where one's faith is brought under the spotlight for further investigation in light of the subject matter under analysis. Here Lartey argues that 'critical consciousness' is allowed to interrogate one's faith. For example, is my faith or tradition able to respond adequately to the real-life experience? The final stage, *'response'*, allows the reflective participants to consider the 'response options' available from the previous stages explored during the cycle. Lartey emphasizes that 'situations are never static' because there is always a constant state of flux. There is always movement in people and situations and he urges the reader: 'Hopefully, one returns with new perspectives; one returns changed as one participates, with others, in transforming moments' (p. 133).

While Lartey's pastoral cycle offers much scope for analysis, a cautionary note is offered by John Colwell. Colwell suggests that a big mistake in doing theological reflection is always starting with the incident. Colwell argues that this is a false starting place because each incident has a context and to start with the concrete experience 'ultimately fails' (Colwell, 2006, p. 215). He reasons that the 'pastoral and ethical goal, after all, is not that we should find ways of responding to problems but that we should be shaped as faithful men and women' (p. 215). We arrive at any situation 'with our baggage, history and stories that contributes to who we are' (p. 216). In terms of theological reflection, he suggests:

> The proper theological question is not how scripture and the Christian tradition might aid me. Rather it is how I, as someone being shaped within the church through its traditions and scriptural stories, respond to the particular dilemma in a manner that is coherent and consistent, trustful and faithful. The Bible functions properly within the Church as a means through which we are shaped and formed as a people who can live trustfully, faithfully, lovingly, hopefully, thankfully, and worshipfully. (Colwell, 2006, p. 216)

Incidents do not occur in a vacuum, but all events culminate in what we understand as the present. Colwell's reasoning is crucial for people who are unclear why they have been shunted to the edges of society due to the colour of their skin, ethnicity, disability, gender, class, or sexuality.

Towards a new paradigm of theological reflection

This model seeks to cultivate a fresh understanding of God in terms not of antidotes and solutions, but rather of healing, deliverance, or transformation (Pattison and Woodward, 2000, pp. 10–12). Models of theological reflection abound, but for my purpose I choose the Eucharist as the biblical lens by which to interpret the episodes and themes of interpersonal conflict. My rationale for choosing this motif is fourfold. First, the Eucharist takes the life, death and Resurrection of Jesus seriously. Second, it encapsulates and honours the uniqueness and sacredness of humanity while acknowledging human catastrophe and despair. Third, the ritual offers the potential for the healing of human suffering and experiencing a new wholeness on earth now. Fourth, for the BMC, there is still a love and respect for the Bible; anything that deals with matters pertaining to the Church and faith from secular sources is disregarded. Furthermore, the Eucharist is not an end in itself, leaving the participants in a state of powerlessness; rather, it is a communal meal in which diverse people can participate and a place where difference finds acceptance. This acceptance is easier said than done when one leaves the comfort and solace of the eucharistic community and ventures into the wider world. Chris Green, in his seminal work *Toward a Pentecostal Theology of the Lord's Supper*, contends that the 'Lord's Supper is a community making meal' and argues for a deeper relationship with 'God and neighbour' by 'grounding the reader in the story of God's redemptive plan of all things' (Green, 2012, pp. 204–7).

In developing this new paradigm, I employ the four-stage model of the Eucharist developed by Dom Gregory Dix. Dix charts the historical development of the Eucharist and its original seven-action scheme to its final four phases, namely, '*took bread*'; '*gave thanks*'; '*the fraction*', the bread is broken; and '*the Eucharist*', the bread and wine are shared (Dix, 2005, p. xvii). I will begin with the first stage of 'taking' or being chosen.

Chosen by God

The Eucharist is a sacred meal shared by those called by God into a relationship with him and other human beings. Every human being has an innate desire to be accepted, yet the word 'chosen' has complications. First, there are the questions such as 'Why have I been chosen to suffer in this way?' Second, if you are being chosen, what is the agenda of the one doing the choosing? Third, being marginalized reinforces the reality of 'not being chosen'. Being chosen, then, is a conflicting, multivalent complexity of existence.

Patti King, commenting on her earlier life experiences, states, 'the word *chosen* felt more like not being chosen', but as an adult she saw 'chosen in a new light; a sacred light, when chosen by God!' (King, 2010, p. 45). Being chosen carries an 'in and out' group mentality. For African Caribbean people, or any socially excluded group, reading the gospel narrative shines new light on their existence, but it depends who is reading the scripture, how it is being read, and the reading strategy employed to read and understand the written text. For example, with a Eurocentric approach, a liberation, feminist, or womanist theological perspective will yield nuanced ways to read the biblical text. From reading the gospel it is evident that Jesus sided with the disinherited (Thurman, 1976). For example, women, lepers, children, the physical and mentally disabled, the 'demon possessed' man in Mark 5, alienated by his community and confused about his identity – all serve as exemplars of people for whom Jesus cared. Siding with the ordinary caused Jesus conflict with the religious and political body of the day. This conflict illustrates the tension encountered when new values or perspectives meet with pre-existent and well-established laws.

For dehumanized people, being chosen by God contrasts with the reality of their lived existence. Marie-France Becker writes, 'Jesus' incarnation remains the way chosen by God to tell us the value that we have in his eyes and thus, to reveal to us our own grandeur' (Becker, 2009, p. 63). This 'grandeur' is not narcissistic, but is where people have a sense of their value, worth and mystery as being created in the image of God (Hall, 2013, p. 225).

Being chosen by God has further significance for excluded individuals because it recognizes equality with all people. Womanist theologian Diana Hayes attests, 'all the people of God, all Christians, see themselves as anointed, chosen by God to serve all of God's creation' (Hayes, 2011, p. 77). Yet being chosen amidst the brutality of human existence can seem surreal. In this regard Thomas Keating observes the following:

We are favoured people. Paul's reading, 'we have been chosen by God for the praise of his glory …' There must be some mistake. It can't be me that God has chosen. It can't be me for whom God's son has died. It can't be me whose sins are all forgiven through the blood of Christ. It can't be me who has eternal life. It cannot be me who has been given divine sonship, the indwelling of the Holy Spirit, victory over sin, and union with all the persons of goodwill. (Keating, 2011, p. 15)

Keating talks of a miracle transcending the negative labelling of insignificance, yet during a conflictive moment one's uniqueness and that of the other is often aborted in exchange for personal gain. In an astute observation, Emmanuel Lartey surmises, 'Every human person is in certain respects, like all others, like some others and like no other' (Lartey, 2003, p. 34). Lartey's concept of human uniqueness is largely neglected when human beings enter the arena of conflict, potentially harming each other.

Another example demonstrates Keating's conceptualization. Within Caribbean culture there remains a legacy of enslavement and colonialism called shadeism (Maher, 2012, p. 219). The basis of this belief enforces the notion that the lighter one's shade of skin the greater one's superiority. The importance of believing in one's 'chosen-ness' where there is no competition with the other is paramount in order for the marginalized to be relieved of his/her socially imposed labelling. Leaving the notion of being chosen, I now turn my attention to the matter of bread.

The Bread symbolizing the body of Christ and human existence

Jesus' pedagogical style often involved employing ordinary objects to demonstrate spiritual truths. One of the ways Jesus symbolized the church fostering an intimate relationship with himself was by breaking bread in remembrance of his sacrificial life and ministry. Bread forms part of the staple diet in many societies, and as Jessica Harren explains, 'bread comes in many forms and shapes: dark, light, coarse, smooth, flat, fluffy, dense, with air bubbles and without, and in many different flavours' (Harren, 2009, p. 288). Accompanying the various shapes of bread is an array of textures, smells and preparations required in its making, further symbolizing the diverse and complex range of humanity. This full acceptance is portrayed as Jesus gathered with the twelve disciples to celebrate the Passover meal. During his time on earth there were numerous disputes among the disciples, yet it was one of the chief ways in which they developed as human beings. Joel Comiskey argues cogently that 'God used conflict to transform his disciples' (Comiskey, 2010, p. 76). Building on Comiskey's comment I acknowledge that in my pastoral practice I could have thought things through and consulted more on certain matters because some of the conflictive episodes were due to latent aspects of my being which would not be revealed until I was in a leadership role and in relationship with the congregation. Here Comiskey posits:

> Conflict often arises as we clash with different personalities and character deficiencies – often the very character deficiencies that annoy us are ones that we share, but sometimes do not recognize. (Comiskey, 2010, p. 696)

It is true to say that conflict can provide the nutrients for personal growth if we dare reflect on matters. For the pastor, such moments are often ignored or avoided, but they are filled with opportunity for gaining personal insights and developing effective ministry.

In gathering around the table for the sacred meal, the sacredness and difficulties of the other cannot be ignored. Harren comments that 'the bread of Eucharist that carried Jesus' body gives us a visible symbol of who can be in church' (Harren, 2009. p. 288). Bread symbolizes the physicality of the human body and participation in the Eucharist makes it an inescapable multisensory experience. From the complications of being chosen it leads to the notion of being blessed.

The Blessing

Jesus' action of taking the ordinary and giving a blessing is significant. The eucharistic scene represents ordinary people created in the image of God, chosen and blessed by him. C. Welton Gaddy states, 'Jesus took bread and blessed it. Ah, the blessing! How every one of us needs a blessing!' (Gaddy, 2005). Harnessing Gaddy's commentary, Dix states that 'to bless a thing, or to give thanks to God for a thing was synonymous in Jewish thought, because in Jewish practice one only blessed a thing by giving thanks to God for it before using it' (Dix, 2005, p. 79). To bless means 'to speak well of, to invoke a benediction upon, to prosper' (Vine, 1996, pp. 132–3). However, it depends on who is doing the speaking and what is taking place in the life of the person being blessed. While an inanimate object such as bread is being prayed for, being blessed often has a positive note, but when one is living in the crucible of suffering it is initially difficult, if not impossible, to comprehend how one can be blessed.

As I have said already, I distance myself from the clichéd and popularized phrase of 'too blessed to be stressed', or 'blessed and highly favoured', uttered in some church circles by Christians and clergy alike as though these words mysteriously anaesthetize and deny the pains of reality (Cook, 1998, p. 4). Examining the life of Jesus as being blessed according to this clichéd understanding is a far cry from the scriptural narrative, where his life demonstrates how being blessed attracts danger. The blessing then is conveyed through words, a visible act belonging to the 'invisible and spiritual realm' allied with spiritual and supernatural power (Prince, 2006, p. 36). The blessing is of such magnitude that Johannes Emminghaus comments, 'Jesus spoke a blessing – the praise of God – over the gifts given to human beings by God, and in this praise and thanksgiving he gave them their new meaning and reality' (Emminghaus, 1997, p. 170). For dehumanized people the blessing transcends degradation and humiliation and elevates them to the state of self-recognition of their God-given humanity.

The Blessing: complicated inclusivity

The Eucharist has far-reaching consequences when observed by oppressed and oppressor alike. For the oppressed, the blessing is a form of healing, but for the oppressor it can continue to affirm their sense of power, with a distorted notion of having a divine right and legitimacy in their subjugation of others.

Words of blessing may be uttered by anyone, but within an African Caribbean religious context, and many other settings where people of African and Asian descent dominate, such sentences carry authority when spoken by the appointed pastor who demonstrates that he cares for the members and considers them as human beings wounded by injurious words, shunted and disturbed by societal attitudes and misunderstandings, marred by the consequences of sin, but still, undeniably, created in the image of God.

Like being chosen, the blessing carries its own set of complications. The blessing is for all who desire to receive the Eucharist, but even among marginalized groups there can exist levels of hierarchy where other marginalized groups are seen as less by the 'higher' within the oppressed groups. Think, for example, of the point made earlier about shadeism. Around the eucharistic table the blessing is needed by all, and in God's eyes is granted to all, especially to those whose humanity is seen as suspect in the world. In contrast, Jesus blesses the bread that leads to total acceptability and therefore, we are all blessed, with no one being blessed more than any other.

The issue of acceptability is a point of concern within the eucharistic setting. Diane L. Hayes, reflecting on preaching the 'good news as the bread and wine of life to all those who hunger and thirst for it', writes:

As the church, the people of God, we are a Eucharistic community, one that gathers to live out again and again the sacrifice of Jesus Christ ... If the Eucharistic celebration is not a reflection of all of us – old and young, Black, white, and every colour and every language under the sun, as various in its celebration as the sands of the sea-shore and the stars in the sky – then all else that flows from there will be of little value. (Hayes, 2011, pp. 36–7)

Hayes makes it clear: regardless of who we are and how we might be perceived, the Eucharist is inclusive of all humanity. One must remember that seated around the table for the inaugural meal of this new institution were Peter, who would later deny Jesus, and Judas who would betray him. Jesus was making no mistake by including these two individuals when remembering the Passover and ushering in a new type of celebration, transforming the life of Christendom for ever. Samuel Fountain elaborates on this matter. He notes:

> Although Jesus talks about the betrayal, in John's Gospel Jesus passed the bread and wine before sending Judas on his way of betrayal. Judas was not excluded from the meal of friendship. Friend or foe, the faithful and the betrayer shared the fellowship meal. The meal was not exclusive for the eleven faithful disciples. It included the betrayer. (Fountain, 2008, p. 70)

This ground-breaking meal included all the disciples, and in the reality of everyday life we will have those gathered to participate in the Eucharist who may be at enmity with themselves, others and God.

The second stage of the Eucharist, with its complex meaning of being blessed and its associated complications, leads to the bread being broken by Jesus. This is a violent action destroying the shape of the bread, thus symbolizing the brokenness of the body of Jesus and humanity. Ironically, though, the bread cannot be distributed without first being broken.

The deliberate breaking of the bread

At this stage of the sacrament Jesus takes the bread, and breaks it while uttering the words: 'Take, eat: this is my body, which is broken for you: this do in remembrance of me' (Luke 22.19). In the minds of most people, brokenness means pain, suffering, loss, depression, self-hatred, loss of sense of self and identity, all contributing to human beings' descent into a state of powerlessness, worthlessness and insignificance. Equally, brokenness is not summed up in a word or two when one's existence is marred from one's historical and cultural context. Similarly, many Christians want to skip from the celebration of Palm Sunday to the Resurrection without giving much, or any, thought to the horror and trauma of the Crucifixion or the chronic pain and uncertainty of Holy Saturday. While not advocating dwelling on pain and suffering, one cannot ignore or trivialize the Crucifixion by sanitizing the gospel and redemption and erasing the violence inflicted on Jesus from one's consciousness. With the human proclivity for avoiding discomfort, brokenness is seldom accepted or understood as a potential for growth (Gaddy, 1991, p. 59). No one desires being broken, but life teaches that often items must be broken to release the contents contained within (Young, 2007, p. 76).

Breaking bread symbolizes three movements. First, in some cultures bread is sacred and becomes a symbol of divine reality and life (Staats, 2008, p. 72). Moreover, Gary Staats emphasizes that bread was deemed so sacred that, 'The idea of cutting bread with a knife was rejected by the Jewish family' (p. 72). David P. Gushee agrees that human life is sacred, but says it does not follow a straightforward and natural path. He indicates that humans can be understood as living a form of binary co-existence:

> It seems fairly natural for human beings to designate a royal class, or a beloved mother, or one's fellow citizen, or one's coreligionists, as sacred. But it is not natural, and certainly not routine in human life, to ascribe sacredness to each and every other human being. In fact, indifference toward most

members of our fellow species, with special hatred for a few and special reverence for a different few, seems the common human experience. (Gushee, 2013, pp. 24–5)

In response to Gushee's observation, the sacredness of another human being is often far from one's consciousness, but the Eucharist provides the opportunity to escape the frenetic pace of life and consider one's actions before God, ourselves and each other.

Second, the breaking of bread symbolizes the pain and horror that must be endured before the goodness of the bread is released. Third, there is the necessity of being broken to release a blessing. Frances Young argues, 'As the Spirit of the Living God breaks and moulds each one of us, so the church has to suffer the pain of brokenness so as to be humbled and recognize difference' (Young, 2007, p. 99). Brokenness as a precursor to being a blessing to others is not recognized or acknowledged as a necessary path for ministry. In this regard, Craig Barnes indicates 'the role of the pastor is to find the truth behind the reality' (Barnes, 2009, p. 22). If Barnes is correct, perceiving the truth behind a conflictive episode is no easy feat as the players in the scene are initially subsumed by the emotionality and enormity of their experience. To find the truth behind the reality, in this case, one's brokenness, the actors must admit and surrender to their dilemma at some point, but by doing so they are made vulnerable and exposed, yet in the moment of such susceptibility the process of healing begins. Such healing is not easily attained nor understood by the victor, the vanquished or the observer in a conflictive scene. The mature and insightful observer is in a unique position and can offer hope while a person is in crisis. The paradox of brokenness is this: in the process of deconstruction and reconstruction one may discover an enrichment of self, others and God which could not have been attained in any other way (Harmon, 2007, pp. 5–6). Such lessons are only learnt through reflective introspection of a conflictive episode or receiving the wise counsel of an elder. This reflection can also occur through the medium of personal journalling, as in my own case, but for the congregation a deeper understanding of a conflictive situation can occur through theological reflection or contextual Bible studies. Alternatively, the appropriate wording of the one who leads the Eucharist, incorporating the context of the participants, can help them reconsider their actions around the sacred immediacy of the Lord's Table.

The capacity of being valued and belonging is an innate human feature and is referred to as a theology of vulnerability. The theology of vulnerability proposes that 'there is strength in weakness as demonstrated by the Suffering Servant in Isaiah chapter 52' (Classenns, 2009, p. 221). It is at the Eucharist table that the celebrants are invisibly vulnerable in the company of one another. According to Thomas Reynolds, 'to exist as a finite being is to be contingent and vulnerable' (Reynolds, 2008, p. 18). In commenting on weakness Reynolds remarks:

> Redemption then is a welcoming, and empowering act of divine hospitality. It does not render human beings 'weak' in the sense of passivity, neither does it negate vulnerability by making human beings invulnerable and perfectly whole … so instead of doing away with impairments and the capacity to suffer, redemption transforms vulnerability into Eucharist with God. An entire 'theology of vulnerability' opens up, wherein the marginal and heretofore neglected (i.e., disability) becomes central. (Reynolds, 2008, p. 19)

Reynolds' observations shift the meaning of bad things happening to people by re-examining the narrative of human existence through a lens which has, as its core, the belief that human beings are created in the image of God, and despite being shunted to the edges of society and made impotent, the reconfiguring of their existence from marginal to significant is prominent and cannot be ignored. Vulnerability is seldom sought after, says Brené Brown: 'Because we're trying to beat vulnerability to the punch.' She continues, 'But this has a negative impact, for without vulnerability, there is no love, no belonging, and no joy' (Brown, 2016).

Vulnerability is not a welcome ally and it was this feeling

that the Windrush generation who had established their church in the 1950s were fearful of, and so they guarded against it (Hall, 2013, p. 244). I too, while not a founding member, felt vulnerable and wanted to protect myself. I commented in my pastoral journals:

> In their case, as new understandings of what it meant to be the church emerged, the founding fathers of the church, with a heightened sense of vulnerability, now perceived their creation as under threat. The religious boundaries they had constructed for their safety were being pushed into new territory. I felt vulnerable because I was appointed to a church where many of the members were much older than me, and I had been socialized to respect all my elders. My vulnerability intensified because I was not prepared by the organization to understand the process of change management and the likely repercussions that change can bring. Furthermore, I was, at that point, unaware of the local church's history and the history of the Caribbean people. There was then an unspoken and unacknowledged vulnerability which caused both sides of the congregational fence, laity, and clergy, to view each other with suspicion and susceptibility. (Hall, 2013, p. 245)

What occurred was that the painful human emotion of vulnerability was kept hidden within the self, but was expressed negatively via conflictive episodes. It is a well-known expression and phenomenon that 'hurt people hurt people'. Explaining this phrase Chester Wood notes:

> We encounter people daily who act and react in ways not readily understood. Often the person does not even understand why he or she responds the way they do ... understanding does not mean excusing; we are still accountable for our actions, the hurt we cause others, the hurt we inflict on ourselves; the pain Jesus feels every time we fail. (Wood, 2008, p. 16)

Wood offers a poignant comment about people not knowing why they react in some of the ways they do. It was this lack of understanding on my part that led me to begin keeping a pastoral journal, and even as I reflected on my actions and contributions in the numerous conflictive episodes within the local congregation, I sensed that there were other factors at play. Hence, I continued to research to discover what might lie beneath the tip of the human iceberg of observed behaviour.

With human brokenness being manifested through interpersonal conflict and as a Christian pastor called to shepherd this congregation, what challenged me most was the need for resolution of this dilemma in the hope of a brighter and sustained future. Such a future is possible if people can learn how to use conflict and brokenness in a constructive and wholesome manner. In this way they can share their brokenness as a form of healing for the benefit of others, and it is the process of sharing that we now examine.

Sharing

Jesus took, blessed and broke bread, and shared it among his disciples (1 Corinthians 11.24). Sharing follows on from brokenness, where people are open to the possibility of sharing the fruits of their brokenness. Jessica Harren attests that 'at the Eucharist table, Jesus touches us when his body is broken open for us – broken open to heal us, broken open to bind us to one another, broken open as our churches should be' (Harren, 2009, p. 285). 'Do this in remembrance of me' is a reminder of how Jesus' suffering coexisted with his sharing. Sharing, then, is not a pain-free altruistic endeavour, but rather the result of a willingness to share one's brokenness as a gift to others, as exemplified by Jesus.

Albert Collver argues that the relationship between the Eucharist and the *diakônia* is *sharing* (Collver, 2010, p. 346). But Martin Robra confronts jargonistic language and adds:

The language of sharing is even more basic than any of our theological or ecclesiological concepts, for it is the people's language in an elementary sense. All people know what sharing means ... and they know that fullness of life is only found in sharing life with one another. 'Sharing' is thus a fundamental symbol of life. (Robra, 1994, p. 285)

Sharing epitomizes the ministry of Jesus. The Incarnation is more than sharing in terms of money and material gifts. Such giving can be accomplished at an emotional and safe distance. Eucharistic sharing involves the revealing and imparting of our weakest selves, or at least our weak self, to the other, which also acts as a reminder of the needs of others.

Sharing: the new possibilities of community

Sharing one's brokenness includes the formation of new relationships in an alienating and 'Good Friday world' (Blythe, 2010). The formation of new relationships is referred to as *lex-vivendi* – 'the way we live our lives in relation to the centrepiece of our liturgical prayers and life – the enactment of the Eucharist' (Irwin, 2005, p. 299). With the possibility of new relationships, Inderjit Bhogal poses a challenging question: 'Can God provide a table in the wilderness?' He writes:

Yes, God can provide a table even in a place of oppression and in the presence of 'enemies' and treat you like an honoured guest. But will only prepare a table in order to celebrate where there is freedom from oppression, even if it means providing a table in the wilderness ... where is the wilderness for us, for you, for the church in which you worship and serve? What is the place you dread? The place you avoid? The place you would choose not to visit or live in? Is it that dull, monotonous, boring relationship which you feel oppressive and which is exhausting? Is it that place of work in which you feel unfulfilled, or a new direction you are being pushed into? ... God wants to celebrate with you there. (Bhogal, 2007, p. 224)

Considering Bhogal's reflection, the Eucharist is to be shared where we are. It is important to recall the time of the Passover and the institution of the Eucharist because both occurred when the Israelites where under oppression and persecution. Thus the Eucharist is to be celebrated not in palatial or opulent surroundings only, but in the seat of pain.

God wants not only to celebrate with us in the world we inhabit but also to challenge the participants of the Eucharist with mystery. It is a timely reminder of the complexity of the spiritual life, and that God is with us in difficult, life-threatening situations. Bhogal responds to this:

> The Lord's Table is prepared in the midst of context and realities that threaten life, in contexts we may prefer to avoid. It challenges greed and seeks an end to hunger in a world of plenty. It challenges the scandal of church disunity. It calls for an end to economic structures that create hunger and famine ... It is in the wilderness God teaches much, woos people, calls, affirms, tests, feeds ... a foretaste of the heavenly banquet prepared for all. (Bhogal, 2007, p. 246)

Bhogal's comment reminds the participants at the Eucharist to take their eyes off their personal dilemmas and gaze upon the world in which they live. The unseen focus of conflict, the assertion of self, can be abated as we take our eyes off our personal needs and consider the needs and humanity of others. In this regard, to participate in the Eucharist is a solemn call to action in the world.

In the light of the Eucharist, sharing can be understood in various ways. First, one of the greatest gifts is to give oneself to another. Second, sharing oneself with others increases the possibilities of others being beneficiaries of the gift of Christ for their liberation, freedom, resurrection, ascension and empowerment by the Spirit in the kingdom of God. Third, sharing acts as a potent healer. The violent and conflicting past of African Caribbean people, manifested as a form of human fragmentation, can be ameliorated through eucharistic encounters if African Caribbean people acknowledge their brokenness and seek their healing. Yet the act of sharing opens oneself to face rejection, even at the Lord's Table.

Miroslav Volf, theologian, speaking as one who had experienced the horrors of wars in the former Yugoslavia and the devastation of ethnic cleansing, contributes to a deepening understanding of conflict and sharing oneself. He refers to exclusion as keeping someone or an entity 'out' from the main circle, but states 'it occurs when the violence of expulsion, assimilation and the indifference of abandonment replaces the dynamics of taking in and keeping out as well as the mutuality of giving and receiving' (Volf, 1996, p. 67). Volf, developing a way forward, refuses to use the terms oppressed and oppressor because he considers them ill-suited to bringing about reconciliation and sustaining peace between people and people groups. Using the work of Gustavo Gutiérrez, he responds, 'The ultimate goal for human beings is love' (Gutiérrez, 1998, p. xxxviii). Building on Gutiérrez's thoughts, Volf develops, in contrast to exclusion, a theology of embrace that comprises 'repentance' and 'forgiveness', 'making space in one-self for the other', and 'healing memory' as pivotal moments in the movement from exclusion to embrace (Volf, 1996, p. 100). This point requires further consideration. Volf's exclusion and embrace, and the expression of sharing, involve risk. Alicia Batten, citing the work of one of her students who was working in an AIDS hospice, and frustrated that her student's work was unacknowledged by the residents of the hospice, wrote, 'To truly serve, one must reach out when the response is uncertain because as Jesus said, "if you love those who love you, what credit is that to you"' (Batten, 2005, p. 110). The eucharistic sharing is not straightforward and even in the act of trying to find resolution, one's offering can be rejected.

Building on the thoughts of Bhogal and Volf, I want to suggest that sharing in the Eucharist lends itself to a reinforcing of the incarnational ministry of Christ, with the potential for liberation for periphery people and oppressors alike.

Eucharistic reconsiderations

The instituting of this mysterious meal was not designed as a one-time or annual event commemorating the Crucifixion and Resurrection of Jesus. Rather, Jesus uttered these sobering words before he left the disparate community of the disciples and gave his life willingly on a wooden cross. 'Do this in remembrance of me.' These words reverberate throughout the world when Christians gather around the Lord's Table to partake of his body and blood. Remembering occurs when something is brought to one's consciousness, but in recent times remembering has become more complicated because much remembering occurs outside the human body. Edward Cassey asserts: 'Human memory has now become self-externalized: projected outside themselves into non-human machines' (Cassey, 2000, p. 2). Computers can 'only store items'; in the end human memories can only be stored by human beings, but for the 'most part, we have increasingly disclaimed responsibilities for them' (p. 2). Remembering is now complex, and despite the distancing from personal responsibility, 'Do this in remembrance of me' draws the participant into a multisensory experience engaging the memory.

Anamnesis as counter memory for Black liberation

The phrase 'Do this in remembrance of me' invites the participants in the Eucharist to remember the life, work, death, burial and Resurrection of Jesus. Acknowledging the context of the Eucharist, the celebration and observance of the Passover amidst the persecution and oppression of the Jewish diaspora, adds personal relevance to the sacrament for marginalized people. *Anamnesis* describes a special remembering 'intended to move a sacred person or event from the past into the present' (McClure, 2003, pp. 16–17). Helen Blier argues that 'the function of *anamnesis* is to draw the congregation back into the primal story of Christianity' (Blier, n.d). Another writer, Julie Gittoes, acknowledges *anamnesis* and describes it as 'The integration of historical, sacramental and ecclesial embodiment of Christ'. She writes:

> The Eucharist looks back at the saving event of Christ's life, death and resurrection. Through it, the church is nourished with the body of Christ; participating in the anticipation of the eschatological fulfilment of God's kingdom. (Gittoes, 2008, front flap)

Gittoes offers a generic understanding of *anamnesis*, relating to the salvific work of Jesus, but Dale Andrews, commenting from an African American location, asserts:

> In creating churches that will connect with its Christian eschatological identity the Black Majority Church faces a complicated task. Any construction in the West risks the exclusion of the particular life and faith struggles of African-Americans ... the Black Majority Church and Black theology has to turn to his/her historical and cultural experiences with Christianity. (Andrews, 2002, p. 98)

Andrews partially concurs with the thoughts of Blier and Gittoes, but he presses for a theology that is relevant and reflects the experience of Black diasporan Christians. Thus returning to the historical experiences is the point of *anamnesis*; the memory or recovery of past experiences to bring them into the present. *Anamnesis* attempts to represent meaning that remains open to new meaning (p. 99). Andrews' Black perspective on Christianity is applicable for the development of BMCs in the UK and his notion of Black experience being a substantial ground for pastoral reflection and pastoral theology is supported by the work of Charles Taylor (1992, pp. 27–34), who attests:

> Black experience can be a source for pastoral theology because it is outside the Euro-American liberal protestant ghetto – yet has ties to it. Second, African-Americans have unique resources for this dialogue because of our 'double consciousness'. (Taylor, 1992, p. 28)

Taylor's remarks reinforce the focus of my doctoral thesis, that interpersonal conflict and the intensity and severity of it experienced in the worshipping African Caribbean community is not only an unpleasant feature of a church community. In addition, it is not an end in itself, but rather it provides possibilities for exploration to bring about empowerment and a new sense of wholeness.

Another writer explaining *anamnesis* is Luke Timothy Johnson. He describes the existential importance of *anamnesis* as a recollection of the past enlivening and empowering the present (Johnson, 1999, pp. 125–7). His analysis of the Eucharist is more than eating bread and drinking wine. It is bound up in identity, a crucial element in the lives of exilic church members and other exilic communities. He observes:

> *Memory* such as this is intimately bound up with the *identity* of both individuals and communities. An individual's story defines one as a person. The myth of a people defines it as a community. Individual or communal *Anamnesia* is a terrifying phenomenon precisely because *Anamnesis* is identity. Without a past, we have no present and little hope for a future. The early church's identity was bound up with the memory of Jesus. It sought an understanding of its present in his past, just as it was motivated to search out his past by the experience of his presence. (Johnson, 1999, p. 126)

Johnson's analysis describes the tension within many African Caribbean church groups, with the Pentecostals possibly being the most disadvantaged. This is due to historically poor educational opportunities in the Caribbean, and the deliberate propagation of British history, while ignoring Caribbean history within the British colonialist education system. This led to a rejection of self, due to a lack of awareness of their own history. This lack of one's history and sense of self and the complex journey of one's people group to the present leads people to the edge of a precipice of cultural identity and cultural oblivion and leaves them there; a psychological disconnect of huge magnitude.

An important assertion about *anamnesis* is not only for members of the BMC but for the invisible Black members in some White Majority congregations whose life of depersonalization is private but nonetheless real (Dixon, 2008, pp. 302–3). In response to the reality of one's life, Helen Blier comments, '*anamnesis* creates a space for people to draw wisdom from their stories in a way that reminds them who they are and what they are to do' (Blier, n.d., p. 7). In conjunction with Blier's comments, Archie Smith speaks from an African American context:

> *Anamnesis* means remembrance of things past. It is to recollect the forgotten past and to participate in a common memory of hope ... *Anamnesis* is a way of keeping alive the dangerous memory of those who lost his/her lives while struggling for the freedom of others. (Smith, 1987, p. 146)

Smith's comment stresses Black people becoming conscious of their history of suffering and pseudo-speciation. However, in remembering the forgotten past a significant dimension of history that must not be omitted is the richness of history, culture and sophistication that African civilizations enjoyed prior to European enslavement. In remembering their past it is important to guard against reviewing it with a sense of romanticism.

Remembering your suffering is not an opportunity for self-pity, generating blame, hating the oppressor or the one you are in conflict with. Rather, it is a moment not to forget where you have come from, based on the life and work of Christ and the efforts and the lives lost by African ancestors which have made possible the life that African Caribbean people and other Black people live. Remembering also helps those who are enjoying the spiritual benefits of salvation not to forget others who could benefit from experiencing Christ and his love. What makes *anamnesis* problematic for the BMC, apart from its lack of historical knowledge, is the irregularity with which the Eucharist is observed. Here, Mark Sturge observes:

From a theological standpoint it should be pivotal in the church because it deals with issues of holiness, personal renewal and the proclamation of the Lord's death. However, it is one of the most neglected areas in the worship and praxis of the BMCs. It is ironic that one of the most fundamental rites celebrating the death and suffering of Christ has become marginalized to the point of being peripheral to his/her church life. (Sturge, 2005, p. 125)

From Sturge's observations and insights, it is imperative that BMCs become more theologically and contextually adept in the functioning and administration of church life and in particular in observing the Eucharist. Failure to do so has rendered many congregations powerless in dealing with their internal issues and made them impotent where they and other Christians are called to be the salt and light of the world.

Conclusion

Interpersonal conflict is an inescapable human experience that operates on a continuum. Whatever visibly happens in human affairs is the tip of the ontological iceberg or, simply put, the symptoms of a situation. Through prayerful consideration, personal and theological reflection and acknowledgement of one's brokenness, and with academic rigour, a new paradigm, a renewed orthodoxy and praxis can emerge for developing a new model of pastoral theology for marginalized people.

To ensure a continual process of growth and looking forward, the Eucharist must become a focal point for introspection leading to a new sense of self, being and action for the benefit of others. We are encouraged by Jesus' words, 'As often as you do this, do this in remembrance of me.' Similarly, the Apostle Paul writes in 1 Corinthians 11 about observing the Eucharist, 'But let a man examine himself.' The participants in the Eucharist are further reminded, 'If we judge ourselves, we would not be judged' (1 Corinthians 11.28, 31).

Eucharistic reconsideration, therefore, is a sacred meal and

moment that speaks to the heart and mind of all who participate. With this in mind, the gathering at the Lord's Table
cannot be simply eating bread and drinking of wine for the
salvific work of Christ for the congregation or individual
alone. No, it must incorporate the remembrance of a bruised
past, both personal and collective, and the development of a
new community. In one sense observing the Eucharist serves
as an educator in one's development for the benefit of others.
The Eucharist must be utilized as a means of remembrance,
Christian interpersonal development and witness to the wider
community. Tissa Balasuriya's comment is a reminder of the
grave and transformative nature of the Eucharist:

> We may ask ourselves how is it possible that societies call-
> ing themselves Christians can offer the Eucharist weekly, for
> years without improving the relationships among persons in
> it. What would be the meaning of 52 masses offered during
> a year in a city if as a result of it there is no effort at bridging
> the immense gulf separating the rich in his/her mansions and
> the poor in the shanties. (Balasuriya, 1979, p. 21)

In a culture that avoids pain, discomfort and suffering but
delights in pleasure-seeking activities, the Eucharist is a
reminder that you cannot have the fullness of life without a
dimension of suffering. Therefore, to have greater relevance
for the African Caribbean faith community, a reinterpretation
of the eucharistic narrative must be concretized in the daily
lived experiences of its participants. The Eucharist connects
with human despair, not to affirm, sacralize or justify human
misery but to acknowledge its existence and attempt to nullify
it by the participation and empowerment of those who share
in the Eucharist. Reflecting on the historical horror, trauma
and effect of African Caribbean existence will take an entity
transcending human agency to foster a sense of wholeness that
might not be achieved in any other way. By participating in the
Eucharist and reflecting on the body that was chosen, blessed,
broken and shared for all, for the pastor and member alike, a
new wholesome future is possible now and yet to come.

Questions for further reflection

1 'Eucharistic encounter' suggests that the Eucharist can be used to address all marginalized people. If your ministry is in an urban setting where there are multitudes of people who live with their backs against the wall, how might you use the eucharistic service to empower them? If your ministry is not urban based, how do you imagine the Eucharist could be used to empower the marginalized?

2 Alice Walker (2012) wrote, 'healing begins where the wound was made'. The notion of healing is somewhat controversial, however, what are the wounds in your congregation or religious setting where healing needs to occur?

3 Why do you think there seems to be so much controversy around the idea of healing in the modern West?

Bibliography

Andrews, D. (2002), *Practical Theology for Black Churches: Bridging Black Theology and African American Folk Religion*, Louisville, KY: Westminster John Knox Press.

Balasuriya, T. (1979), *The Eucharist and Human Liberation*, London: SCM Press.

Barnes, C. (2009), *The Pastor as Minor Poet: Texts and Subtexts in the Ministerial Life*, Grand Rapids: Wm. B. Eerdmans.

Batten, A. (2005), 'Studying the Historical Jesus through Service', *Teaching Theology and Religion*, 8(2), pp. 107–13.

Becker, M. F. (2009), *15 Days of Prayer with Saint Marie Clare of Assisi*, New York: New York City Press.

Bhogal, I. (2007), 'A Table in the Wilderness (Psalm 78.9)', in Michael Jagessar and Anthony Reddie (eds), *Black Theology in Britain: A Reader*, London: Equinox.

Blier, H. (n.d.), 'Remembering not to Forget: Anamnesis and the Persistence of Vocation', http://old.religiouseducation.net/member/02_papers/blier.pdf (accessed 3.2.2021).

Blythe, M. (2010), Early morning prayers, in 'Sam Sharpe and the Quest of Liberation', Theology and Legacy for Today Conference, Regent's Park College, University of Oxford, 13–16 April 2010.

Brown, B. (2016), 'Daring to be Vulnerable with Brené Brown', https://www.takingcharge.csh.umn.edu/daring-be-vulnerable-brene-brown (accessed 27.1.2021).

Cassey, E. (2000), *Remembering: A Phenomenological Study*, Bloomington, IN: Indiana University Press.

Classenns, L. J. (2009), 'Isaiah', in Gail R. O' Day and David L. Petersen (eds), *Theological Bible Commentary*, Louisville, KY: Westminster John Knox Press.

Collver III, A. B. (2010), 'Works of Mercy and Church Unity: Does Service Unify and Doctrine Divide?', *Concordia Journal*, 36(4), pp. 342–53.

Colwell, J. (2006), 'The Church as Ethical Community', in Paul Ballard and Stephen Holmes (eds), *The Bible in Pastoral Practice: Readings in the Place and Function of Scripture in the Church*, Grand Rapids, MI: Wm. B. Eerdmans.

Comiskey, J. (2009), *The Relational Disciple: How God Uses Community to Shape Followers of Jesus*, Riverside, CA: CCS Publishing.

Cook, D. J. S. (1998), *Too Blessed to be Stressed: Women on the Move*, Nashville: Thomas Nelson.

Dix, G. (2005), *The Shape of the Liturgy*, London: Bloomsbury T & T Clark.

Dixon, L. (2008), 'Tenth Anniversary Reflections on Robert Beckford's *Jesus is Dread: Black Theology and Black Culture in Britain*', *Black Theology: An International Journal*, 6(3), pp. 300–7.

Emminghaus, J. (1997), *The Eucharist: Essence, Form and Celebration*, Collegeville, MN: The Liturgical Press.

Fountain, S. (2008), A *Man for All Time*, New York: Eloquent Books.

Gaddy, C. W. (1991), *A Soul Under Siege: Surviving Clergy Depression*, Louisville, KY: Westminster John Knox Press.

Gaddy, C. W. (2005) 'Transformation', sermon preached in Northminster Baptist Church on 10 April 2005, http://dcommon.bu.edu/xmlui/handle/2144/151 (accessed 17.3.2011).

Gittoes, J. (2008), *Anamnesis and the Eucharist: Contemporary Anglican Approaches*, Aldershot: Ashgate Publishing Limited.

Green, C. (2012), *Toward a Pentecostal Theology of the Lord's Supper: Foretasting the Kingdom*, Tennessee, CPT Press.

Gushee, P. D. (2013), *The Sacredness of Human Life: Why an Ancient Biblical Vision is Key to the World's Future*, Grand Rapids, MI: Wm. B. Eerdmans.

Gutiérrez, G. (1998), *A Liberation of Theology: History, Politics and Salvation*, 2nd edn, Caridad Inda and John Eagleson (trans), New York: Orbis Books.

Hall, D. (2013), 'But God Meant It for Good: Interpersonal Conflict in an African Caribbean Faith Community – A Pastoral Study', unpublished PhD thesis, Birmingham: University of Birmingham.

Harmon, Hugh J. (2007), *Broken, Just to Be Made New*, Columbia: Kingdom Book and Gift LLP.

Harren, Jessica (2009), 'Bread and Bones: Knowing God through the

Communion Table', *Journal of Religion, Disability and Health*, 13(3 & 4), pp. 274–92.

Hayes, L. D. (2011), *Standing in the Shoes My Mother Made Me: A Womanist Theology*, Minneapolis: Ausburg Fortress.

Irwin, K. (2005), *Models of the Eucharist*, Mahwah, NJ: Paulist Press.

Johnson, L. T. (1999), *The Writings of the New Testament: An Interpretation*, revised edn, London: SCM Press.

Keating, T. (2011), *And the Word Was Made Flesh*, New York: Lantern Books.

King, P. (2010), *Acorns from God: God's Word for Personal Growth and Encouragement*, Bloomington, IN: AuthorHouse.

Lartey, E. (2003), *In Living Colour: An Intercultural Approach to Pastoral Care and Counselling*, London: Jessica Kingsley Publishers.

Maher, J. M. (2012), Foreword by I. Parker, *Racism and Cultural Diversity: Cultivating Racial Harmony Through Counselling, Group Analysis, and Psychotherapy*, London: Karnac Books.

McClure, J. (2003), *The Four Codes of Preaching: Rhetorical Strategies*, Louisville: Westminster John Knox Press.

Pattison, S. and Woodward, J. (2000), 'An Introduction to Pastoral and Practical Theology', in James Woodward and Stephen Pattison (eds), *The Blackwell Reader in Pastoral and Practical Theology*, Oxford: Blackwell Publishers.

Prince, D. (2006), *Blessing or Curse: You Can Choose*, Grand Rapids, MI: Chosen Books.

Reynolds, T. (2008), *Vulnerable Communion: A Theology of Disability and Hospitality*, Grand Rapids, MI: Brazos Press.

Robra. M. (1994), 'Theological and Biblical Reflection on Diakonia', *The Ecumenical Review*, 46(3), pp. 276–86.

Smith, A. (1987), 'The Relational Self in the Black Church: From Bondage to Challenge', in Paul W. Pruyser (ed.), *Changing Views of the Human Condition*, Macon, GA: Mercer University Press.

Staats, G. (2008), *Jewish Domestic Customs and Life in Interpreting the Gospels*, self-published.

Sturge, M. (2005), *Look What the Lord has Done! An Exploration of Black Christian Faith in Britain*, Bletchley: Scripture Union.

Taylor, C. (1992), 'Black Experience as a Resource for Pastoral Theology', *Journal of Pastoral Theology*, 2, pp. 27–34.

Thurman, H. (1976), *Jesus and the Disinherited*, Boston, Beacon Press.

Vine, E. V. (1996), *Vine's Expository Dictionary of Old and New Testament Words*, Nashville: Thomas Nelson Publishers.

Volf, M. (1996), *Exclusion and Embrace: A Theological Exploration of Identity, Otherness, and Reconciliation*, Nashville: Abingdon Press.

Walker, A. (2012), *The Way Forward Is with a Broken Heart*, New York: The Ballentine Publishing Group.

Wood, C. W. (2008), *Hurt People, Hurt People: Getting a Grip on Anger*, Maitland, FL: Xulon Press, Incorporated.

Young, Frances (2007), *Brokenness and Blessing: Towards a Biblical Spirituality*, Grand Rapids, MI: Baker Academic.

5

Negative Labelling:
The Product of an Insecure Mind

I am talking of millions of men who have been skilfully injected with fear, inferiority complexes, trepidation, servility, despair, abasement. (Aimé Césaire, *Discours sur le Colonialisme*, in Fanon, 2008, p. 1)

Introduction

In the previous chapter Black humanity was asserted through the lived lens and eucharistic sacrament on the Jamaican plantations during the transatlantic slave trade. It is now time to explore what it means to have a Black identity in the UK, created and owned by the former colonial subjects.

For centuries, African diasporan people have known little else other than being dominated. This is made clear by Michael Gomez in *Reversing the Sail*, where he refers to the invasion of Africa by Europeans for enslavement purposes, beginning from 1441 (Gomez, 2005, pp. 59–81). First, it was enslavement and then, after its abolition in 1807, colonialism. The author contends that Black folk remain in a mental bondage to enslavement. Psychological enslavement is conceptualized by Frantz Fanon in *Black Skin, White Masks* when he states:

> The black man has no ontological resistance in the eyes of the white man. Overnight, the Negro has been given two frames of reference within which he has been placed. His metaphysics, or, less pretentiously, his customs and the sources on which they were based, were wiped out because they were

in conflict with a civilization not created for black people. (Fanon, 2008, p. 83)

This notion of mental slavery was commented on in song by the late Bob Marley, who sang in his famous 'Redemption Song', 'emancipate yourself from mental slavery (Marley, 1980).

New arrivals

Three years after the Second World War, 492 people from the Caribbean arrived in England on the *Empire Windrush* (Reddie, 2006, p. 13). They arrived from colonial rule within the West Indies, and experienced further oppression, despite the appealing advertisements in the Caribbean: 'Further your Ambitions – Go to England' (Hill, 1958, p. 19). In the Caribbean, Black folk were treated and affirmed as human beings; however, this was not the case in Britain (p. 14). When they arrived, they came motivated to aspire to, accept and integrate into a British lifestyle. Clifford Hill confirms this when he writes, 'the Caribbean has grown up with a high regard for the Englishman, and it is one of his ambitions to live like the Englishman does' (p. 22). The Caribbean came to Britain with an understanding of being Caribbean and a British subject and desiring to be treated as a fellow human being but was met with hostility.

The counter argument to this is 'You have a roof over your head and food on the table, what more could you possibly want?' (personal conversation, 2008). The question is posed, if someone wants to be treated with dignity, do they have a chip on their shoulder? Being treated fairly as a human being is a universal human instinct. It could be said that there is no evidence to support what I am saying, but I do not agree, given the current state of injustice throughout the world. What follows is a personal reflection, shaped by living in England, and it is undoubtedly biased. But nonetheless it is a lived experience.

Defining terms

The term 'Black' is not easily defined and, contrary to opinion, it does not have a fixed meaning. Robert Beckford in *Dread and Pentecostal* defines Black as 'a complex ethno-political description serving two purposes. First, it describes black skinned African people. Second, it describes non-white or those engaging in resistance to dominance' (Beckford, 2000, p. 2). Chigor Chike in 'Black Theology in Britain – One Decade On', referring to the notion of Black, cites Emmanuel Lartey's understanding as not only meaning African American folk, but 'integrating the voices of African, Caribbean and Asian people as well as those who identify with "the Black experience" in terms of heritage, oppression and domination' (Lartey, 1999, p. 81). Social activists also use Black in a wider, political sense that includes Asians and other people who might be described as 'ethnic minority' (Chike, 2006, pp. 192–209). Chike expands the term Black when he uses the definition employed in the 2003 Racial Justice Sunday pack, where it describes Black as 'anyone facing discrimination on the basis of skin colour, whether of African, Asian or Afro-Caribbean origin' (p. 1). To add a further complexity, Kate Coleman in 'Another Kind of Black' theorizes that Blackness is *Mettisage*, which focuses on Black British women in French anthropological and literary terms and, as she argues, this can be used as a tool for cultural discourse (Coleman, 2007).

What is problematic is whether people who are categorized as Black actually understand themselves as Black. For example, growing up in Leicester in the 1970s and 1980s Asians did not see themselves as Black. Such an identity was associated with being dark skinned, Africans, servile coupled with poor education. Since I originally wrote this chapter a new expression of Black, Asian, Minority Ethnic (BAME) is now the politically correct term in homogenizing all minority groups (Equality Act 2010). To reaffirm this definition, I refer to Black as being those individuals who were severed from their birth lands and have the shared cultural history that contains the Middle Passage.

In understanding faith, a description is required. Clifford Hill states in *Black and White in Harmony* that 'more than 95 per cent of people in Jamaica go to church, and are deeply religious' (Hill, 1958, pp. 19–21). Faith and its importance are developed by Anthony Reddie in *Black Theology in Transatlantic Dialogue*: 'the importance of faith, or rather religious knowledge, is inextricably linked to personal holistic growth' (Reddie, 2006, p. 10). Yet this is not the whole picture. It would be incorrect to assume, in terms of faith, that all Black people are the same, or that all, or 95 per cent, of Black people in Britain go to church. Black people are not homogenous in their worldview and faith perspective. However, in this chapter, I will locate faith within the Black Christian church movement in Britain. By this I mean churches within any denomination where the majority of the leadership and congregation are African Caribbean or descendants within the African Caribbean diaspora (Sturge, 2005, p. 31).

Living in Britain

In beginning this chapter, a poignant question must be asked. What will it take for White hegemony to acknowledge, accept and challenge their advantages and observe the effect they have had on Caribbean diasporan people, or any other non-White person (Reddie, 2006, p. 65)? White hegemony is not about to give up its power nor its self-ascribed importance, and Black folk, having been marginalized by White supremacy, must ask: how can the dominant powers speak for us, when they are scared and unwilling to acknowledge Black folk's experience and view the world from their position? This reluctance or inability to engage with such experience is alluded to in David Isiorho's 'Black Theology in Urban Shadow', where he cogently states: 'For the English, to confront and deal with racism and the racializing process is to erode the national concepts of superiority that centuries of aggressive colonialism have embedded deep within the national psyche' (Isiorho, 2002, p. 47).

Isiorho does not leave it there, but further compounds the issue when he comments, in moving forward, that high-ranking officials in the Church of England are challenged in being more accommodating to Black people (Isiorho, 2002). To erode a power base is no easy feat and raises emotive uncomfortableness in the powerful. Before dominant voices can comment on Black experience, they must at least attempt to acknowledge the world as Black folk express it, not a world of ideas, theories, and abstract notions, but the world of feeling, sensation and experience, and the effect it has on one's thinking and self-regard. Also, if White hegemony can muster the courage to critique itself and come close to Blackness, with an openness to glimpse what Black folk feel, they can then, and only then, comment.

The problem with White people entering a world alien to them is reinforced by James Perkinson in *White Theology* when he writes about the 'experience gulf' existing between the Black and White worlds. The world of Black experience, of racial oppression and the struggle against it, must necessarily be comprehended as irremediably 'other' if it is not (yet one more time) to be reductively annexed to White experience and distorted by White theory (Perkinson, 2004, p.38). Perkinson states that for White people to sense Black experience they must encounter a 'reverse minoritization' in which for an extended period they occupy the place of the racial 'other' without relief. This could accomplish a full initiation into the deeper meaning of race (p. 46).

Black folk in the West enter a Whiteness world daily through schools, literature, work, media and education. The environment oozes Whiteness and enhances White supremacy, yet Black folk are unable to stay in it for too long because it demeans who they are. If they stay too long, they are unsure how it will affect their wellbeing. 'Your world is brilliant with its cerebral dominance and its varied cognitions, but it fails to soothe the pain' – this is how so many Black people feel living in a society restricting and distorting Black humanity. Some have learnt to straddle two existent worlds, as articulated by W. E. B. Du Bois in his conceptualization of 'Double Consciousness' in

The Souls of Black Folk. Here Du Bois describes his existence as a Black man in a White society: 'It dawned upon me with a certain suddenness that I was different from the others; or like, mayhap, in heart and life and longing, but shut out from their world by a vast veil' (Du Bois, 2012, p. 2). In order to 'keep our heads', Black folks have to retreat into a world or space to stay sane. This place of existential refuge is articulated by Lorraine Dixon in 'A Reflection on Black Identity and Belonging in the Context of the Anglican Church in England'. Despite being born and educated in Britain, and being a member of the Anglican Church, the only place she felt comfortable was at home, or with her Black peers, listening to Black music, eating cultural food, and hearing stories from the Caribbean from her parents' generation (Dixon, 2000, pp. 22–7). Dixon articulates a common experience, where Black people must find spaces where healing and remaining sane is possible, coupled with places aiding self-discovery that they are unable to find elsewhere (p. 27).

Such ideas may make some African, Asian, Caribbean diasporan people and White people feel uncomfortable, but if we begin to address the 'uncomfortableness' we may get somewhere. 'Let us not offend', we are told. Yet too often, stoic politeness and political correctness cause important and 'troubling' issues to be avoided. It is impossible to speak for the White person's experience, but there remain suspicion and discomforting experiences in both ethnic camps, the White person with their feelings of superiority and guilt and the Black person with feelings of inferiority and shame. White persons are not quick to divest themselves of their privilege, and Black persons do not know how to rid themselves of their pain of inferiority and shame.

What's in a name?

The adage, 'Sticks and stones may break my bones, but words will never hurt me' flies in the face of how words or language are used to categorize and psychologically wound people. For example, defining the term 'Black' does not fully encapsulate the meaning of the word and its historical implications for those who have been labelled as such and have been burdened with its connotations. The term *labelling* was coined by Howard Becker in *Outsiders: Studies in the Sociology of Deviance*. While Becker's focus was criminology and deviance, the term can be applied to our subject area. Becker defined labelling as 'social rules constructed, and then they are broken. The one who breaks the social rules is labelled as an "outsider"' (Becker, 1963, p. 1). Another interpretation of labelling is stated by Roger Smith in *Youth Justice*. Smith defines 'labelling theory' as the potential consequences in setting individuals apart on an attitudinal basis (Smith, 2007, p. 67). A disturbing aspect of labelling is singling out people who appear to represent a threat. Thus, concentrating interventions on them may in effect create a self-fulfilling expectation because they live up to the label applied (p. 68).

The question may be asked, 'Why should we be defined by two negative statements?' The term Black has had a long, convoluted and negative history and continues to influence English language and thought. For example, 'black devils', 'black Friday', 'the black sheep of the family', 'a black day', or something that is 'hanging over me like a black cloud'. The power of language to influence the mind of the speaker and hearers cannot be overestimated. In Christian terms, we are all born equal and created in the image of God, but the labelling and subsequent treatment of Black people betray biblical descriptions. I am aware of other marginalized groups of people – gays, trans people, disabled people and women – but this chapter will be limited to exploring the plight of African Caribbean diasporan people.

The purpose of labelling

That Black people did not invade the shores of Britain to conquer the nation is a statement of fact. Neither did non-European contact disturb or disrupt White identities (Bonnett,

2000, p. 14). Caribbean people came to Britain by invitation and as guests, willing to please their hosts (Hill, 1958, p. 101). The newcomers arrived in Britain as British subjects carrying a historical legacy of enslavement and colonialization. Now they were entering into the arena where the hosts were purveyor of White supremacy, espousing an ideology that categorized Black people negatively. To help us understand we need to reflect on two critical questions: why have Black people been labelled as such, and what have they done to White folk to warrant such behaviour and treatment?

As reflection continues, it leads us to ask the question, how much does the pejorative projection onto black bodies reveal the English psyche's darker side, and how much does it reflect racial intolerance in Britain? Other questions emerge: a highly visible colour is labelled, yet those same folk are made invisible in many historical accounts and areas of influence, with limited access to privileges within the British landscape. What have Black folk done? Why must they be so hidden?

It would appear that black bodies in Britain disturb the national psyche – a mind which, over centuries, has deposited violence and psychological toxin on other shores, and has its own history of attempting to expel Black people from its land (Kaufman, 2018). The various invitations and expulsions – and attempted expulsions – experienced by Black people in Britain suggest a nation characterized by an ongoing relational dislike and dysfunction. Despite its rhetoric and illusion of self-aggrandizement, there remains a sense of 'dis-ease' with itself, projected onto the 'other'. An unsure and insecure mind that must avoid or eliminate anything that seems to pose a threat, real or perceived. If you cannot eliminate the threat, disempower it. And what better way to do this than to expose it to psychological violence, robbing the perceived threat's identity and rendering it powerless to know who it is and who it might become?

The effect of labelling

Labelling is more than words. It is, as indicated, a powerful controlling force to dominate people. During a lecture, social scientist Joy DeGruy (2006), commenting on her publication *Post Traumatic Slave Syndrome*, was asked a question about the horrors of the Middle Passage. How was it possible to justify treating another human being in such cruel ways? She responded by saying that there is a phenomenon called dissonance. By this she meant that if you rename something from what it is, you can then treat it how you like.

Labelling has two detrimental effects on its victims. First, it causes people to become outsiders (Becker, 1963, p. 1). Second, it causes its victims to take on the mantle of inferiority, or, as Becker expresses it, 'the person is seen as deviant as defined by the person who has made the rule' (p. 3).

Gus John in *The New Black Presence in Britain* argues cogently that 'black people in Britain, when they first arrived were not the problem, but their presence highlighted fissures that were deeply rooted in British society' (John, 1976, p. 19). What might these fissures be, and what might we discover in Britain's collective unconscious if it was placed in the psychiatrist's chair for analysis? What might the presenting problem be leading such a mind to come for therapy?

The presenting problem is the initial reason or cause why people seek a therapist. In this case, the problem might be the impulses behind the negative labelling projected onto Black people who desire nothing more than being treated as human beings.

The national psyche in the psychiatrist's chair

The collective unconscious was conceptualized by the depth psychologist Carl Jung. Jung believed that the collective unconscious was what the ancients called 'the sympathy of all things' (Jung, 1974, p. 160). The definition is complex. Frieda Fordham, in *An Introduction to Jung's Psychology*, states that 'to define the collective unconscious is to attempt the impossible, for we can have no knowledge either of its boundaries or its true nature; all that we can do is to observe its manifestations, describe them, and try to understand them as far as possible' (Fordham, 1966, p. 27).

If such thoughts regarding insecurity or anxiety and its effects are true, what does the English psyche have to be insecure about? This unspoken but felt awkwardness is a reminder, and should inform us as Black people, that despite the intimidating voice of White hegemony, all is not well with them or us. James Perkinson, in *White Theology* (2004), conceptualizes a scenario that will help to analyse White supremacy/the White psyche in the psychiatrist's chair. Therapy invites us to look at ourselves and our associated distresses and neuroses. However, in this case, it may prove difficult as this client is being counselled under duress, and clients forced to go for counselling are generally resistant and uncooperative. Perkinson expresses a similar viewpoint:

> It is fundamentally a structure of denial. It is elusive to talk about, as we have noted, precisely in its function of hiding history and domination under a presumed normalcy and naturalized superiority. What has been hidden is its history of exploiting and oppressing people of colour remains largely opaque – ungrasped and unfelt by white people. (Perkinson, 2004, pp. 175–6)

Visiting Edinburgh Castle and hearing about the wars and invasions between the Scots and the English reveals an interesting sub-story. It appears that the English cannot help themselves. They have a proclivity to dominate, override and control others. Yet another reading might indicate insecure behaviour as a survival instinct.

White insecurity/White fragility and its characteristics

What is still noticeable is the literature dealing with the effect of Whiteness and its consequences on Black and White life in England, although some would have us believe that there are no race issues in the UK. In 'Anti-Black Racism, Self-Esteem, and the Adjustment of White Students in Higher Education', authors Garriott, Love and Tyler (2008) argue that 'there are psychological consequences on White people due to racism. For them, racism has consistently been identified as benefiting whites having superior ways of being.' However, recent findings suggest that there is a negative 'cost' to White people. The authors cite such costs or experiences as guilt, fear and anxiety, limited social relationships, and a distortion of how the self and others are seen. In having a distorted view of others, people may be puzzled as to whether colour blindness is a characteristic of insecurity manifesting itself through denial. They must ask a simple question, 'How can you not see when someone is Black?'

Colour blindness – really?

Maybe not seeing colour is a way forward for integration and so forth, but not seeing colour is puzzling. How is it not possible to see a Black person? If something is good you want to see it. Why, then, should Black people be ignored, dismissed, neglected and hidden? Again, is colour blindness a psychological dysfunction attempting to soothe or eliminate emotions of discomfort for White people? Is colour blindness used simultaneously as a form of social control or social acceptance, so that Black people can feel at ease and not cause too much trouble and White folk do not have to feel uncomfortable in their presence?

If you push some White folk by asking what they mean by 'they do not see colour', they get defensive and respond by quipping, 'Black folk are causing trouble.' If you do not see Blackness, you render Black people invisible, insignificant and unimportant. If you do not see Blackness, you will not consider that Black folk are human beings created in the image of God and you will not value them. If you do not see colour, you ignore their specialness, their culture and their rich history. If you do not see colour, you miss the many Black inventors and scientists who have lived and contributed to the development of civilizations throughout the world. If you ignore Black folk, you do so at your peril. If you ignore Black folk, you remain imprisoned in your castle of White supremacy, dominance and power and you remain far from yourself and from life.

While the White psyche is being analysed and hopefully healed by in-depth introspection, the victim is brought into the counselling room as the non-present client. People from the diaspora are termed dislocated, and this notion needs developing. Dislocation suggests pain and reflects the idea that a joint needs repositioning. Even after repositioning the surrounding area can still be painful and tender to touch for some time, and remains a point of weakness. For many African Caribbean people, especially those born in the UK, it is not so much dislocation but rather a fracture. In fracturing, resetting the bones can also be painful. On occasions, where there has been a partial fracture, a surgeon has to completely break the bone and reset it so that it heals properly. While these are metaphors, in one sense they describe the problem faced by many African Caribbean people in the UK: they are fractured, but do not know they are fractured and are thus unable to be healed.

'Let us not offend', some may say. But notice a strange phenomenon. Every nation, it seems, has the liberty, freedom and confidence to express who they are. So there is some perplexity as to why African Caribbean diasporan people tend to compromise or are unclear about who they are. It is as though they have colluded with the oppressor and in doing so are rendered powerless, having internalized feelings of fear from those who fear them. The next story illustrates this point.

At a conference at the end of 2007, a conversation ensued with a Black man of Caribbean heritage born in the UK. As the conversation continued, he said he was English and had no affiliation or affinity with the Caribbean whatsoever. The listeners were left puzzled, but why should they be? There are some Black folk who have such feelings. It could be that for some, matters about ethnicity, race and culture are of no concern. Some have chosen to bury their heads in the sand, perhaps because they find it difficult to understand who they are, and beginning to reconnect with themselves is hard, painful work.

With negative labelling coming from an insecure mind, we shall now consider a possible antidote to the toxicity of such negative descriptions and what is needed to bring people to life who have, by and large, internalized the oppressor's energy. The Black liberation theologian Anthony Reddie hits the nail on the head when he states, 'to be black in Britain is to have one's experiences, history and realities ignored, disparaged, and ridiculed' (Reddie, 2006, pp. 12–13). He continues, 'being black in the twenty-first-century Britain and the wider world is to discover what you know is dismissed as untrue and without any political, cultural or theological consequence' (p. 13).

'Renaming' one's Black self – autonomous identity

The first section of this chapter wrestled with the projected negative labelling due to the myths and inaccuracies surrounding Black humanity. While this chapter does not deal with neurobiology, physiology or the endocrine system, we must bear in mind that living in a state of fear and having one's humanity exposed to constant threat, whether real or perceived, produces high levels of stress while simultaneously playing havoc in the traumatized body (Van Der Kolk, 2014). Regaining power, therefore, for the Black beings who are into defining who they are will have significant effects on their well-being. At this point it is important to change terms.

A label is a small piece of paper, fabric, plastic, or similar material attached to an object and giving information about it. Whereas a name refers to a word or set of words by which a person or thing is known, addressed or referred to. This is important. Black folk have had labels attached to them for centuries. Labels are external references or additions which someone must put on or attach to an object. A name, on the other hand, is how one is known, personable, relatable, a living being who has life, energy and potential.

As the black body is dehumanized, what can be done to redeem, resurrect or 're-label' the Black self? In other words, how can the black body be 'undemonized?' One thing is certain; Black self-development and identity cannot be left to anyone else. Self-determination, and in this case 'renaming the Black self', is echoed by Marcus Garvey in *The Philosophy and Opinions of Marcus Garvey, or Africa for the Africans*: 'As a people, we can expect very little from the efforts of present-day statesmen of other races' (Garvey, 2013, p. 36).

Before we consider theological themes, we need to explore other sources to aid understanding of self-naming Black humanity.

There is a universality and interconnectedness with Blackness. The self-ascribing of a name is not, as Sudhi Rajiv articulates in *Forms of Black Consciousness* (1992), where 'The white self-concept can exist independent of the larger community whereas the Black self is deeply entrenched in their collective experience of his race' (p. 32). The beginning of our transformation starting in our minds is not a new idea. Chancellor Williams, in *The Destruction of Black Civilization* (1987), stresses, 'The liberation of our minds is task number one. It will not be easy and will not be easily achieved in a single generation' (p. 331).

The renewing of the mind is the birthing of a new self. Re-creating a new self is imperative for people of African descent and transcends simply acquiring African names. Although there are counter arguments to this idea, what tends to be a common factor if you ask African people what their names mean, whether they were born in Africa or not, is that without fail they know the meaning of their name. So what's in a name? Molefi Kete Asante in *Afrocentricity* argues for people to take an African name. He contends that 'for most African Americans' (and I daresay also for African Caribbean people living in the UK), 'their names are remnants of the slave master's names'

(Asante, 2003, p. 38). For example, 'Washington, Jefferson, Lincoln, Bennett and others' (p. 38). Asante continues:

> After emancipation, the majority of Africans had to choose another name for legal and social purposes ... having little knowledge about Africa they chose names they heard and were common around them. Some, however, resisted the imposition of white names and selected names that they thought were African. (Asante, 2003, p. 38)

Thus, having had an important aspect of the African's identity ripped away by the ravages of enslavement, the former enslaved were now left with the task of recreating their own identity. Examples of Black people who changed their names are Malcolm Little who changed his name to Malcolm X because, according to Saladin Amber, 'His transformation represented a kind of double freedom – becoming X was freedom from white identities and familial ties.' Furthermore, 'becoming El-Hajj Malik El- Shabazz was a freedom from organizational orthodoxy within the Nation of Islam and its deviation from acceptable Islamic teaching' (Amber, 2014, p. 73). Other examples include Stokely Carmichael who changed his name to Kwame Ture in honour of two early proponents of Pan-Africanism, Ghanaian Kwame Nkrumah and Guinean Sékou Touré. Asante states, 'Defined by whites as "negroes" and identified by white names, they were bodies without spirits, people without dignity, whether they knew it or not' (Asante, 2003, p. 38). He further reinforces the idea:

> When you are circumscribed by someone else you cannot have a healthy respect for yourself as a person. Furthermore, the essence of psychological health is that one deals and is capable of dealing with his [sic] identity. If we are unable to deal with our identity, we are unable to come to terms with consciousness. (Asante, 2003, p. 38)

Asante makes a strong case for acquiring African names to help how we perceive ourselves and how others perceive us.

To exchange Eurocentric names for African names is traumatic and fearful for many Black people and dramatic for White people. The point Asante makes is worth pursuing through the lens of Black consciousness.

In *Black Consciousness*, the Black South African political activist Steve Biko begins by saying how we are having to 'deal with a problem we did not create' (Biko, 1978, p. 87). Black consciousness, he cogently asserts, 'is due because of a deliberate creation of humanity, whether by an act of God, or the artificial fabrication of the truth by power hungry people whose motive is authority, security, wealth and comfort' (p. 87).

Biko concurs with the writers who advocate that Blacks must formulate thoughts without guidance and trusteeships from White people. Biko uses Marxist theory as a tool to create a Black consciousness. The thesis, he posits, is strong White racism. The antithesis is strong Black solidarity among the Blacks on whom this White supremacy is seen to prey (Biko, 1987, p. 90). The principle supporting Black consciousness is 'a continuous struggle for truth; therefore, we have to examine and question old concepts, values and systems, creating/evaluating schemes, forms and strategies' (p. 92).

Negative labelling had its inception in the mind of the enslavers and was then projected onto the enslaved, coupled, in many instances, with Christianity being used to justify such an institution. The faith used to enslave was later reappropriated by many African ancestors, yet in many respects they did not go far enough. Biko argues that Christianity must be re-examined through a Black theology lens. He calls for 'Christ as a fighting God and not a passive one who allows a lie to rest unchallenged'. Black theology, he claims, 'grapples with existential issues and does not claim to be a theology of absolutes' (p. 94). Biko's most challenging argument urges priests and ministers to save Christianity by adopting a Black theological approach and thereby once more uniting the Black man with his God (p. 94).

An earlier question posited whether Black people can be 'undemonized'. Such a quest will be a work lasting several generations, but once begun it must continue for the future of all African diasporan people. Biko cogently states:

One writer states, colonialism is never satisfied with having the native in its grip but, by some strange logic, it must turn to its past and disfigure and distort it. Hence the history of the black man [sic] is most disappointing to read. All major characters who created societies and civilizations are effectively demonized. Therefore, we must give heed to our history and it must be rewritten with characters in their rightful place. (Biko, 1987, p. 9)

In addition, Biko maintains that 'culture must be defined in concrete terms and we must relate the past to the present and demonstrate a historical evolution of man [sic]'. Finally, he suggests that a communal aspect of community is essential to humanity. That is, a 'man [sic] centred society manifesting a sacred tradition of sharing' (p. 10). This sharing symbolizes a total involvement and not fragmented groups. This involvement leads to offering the greatest gift possible, which is a more human face.

Considering theological aspects of naming, Black British womanist Kate Coleman argues for a process in naming as she reflects in 'Being Human: A Black British Christian Woman's Perspective'. She comments:

As in Jewish and many African societies, naming is less an imposition of identity, than an act of incorporation. It is a recognition of individuality, defining the child's personality, affirming her or his destiny and establishing her or his status in the family. Within these contexts a name shapes one's self understanding, providing descriptive information about the circumstances of births or traits emerging in the character of a child. (Coleman, 2007, p. 163)

Coleman illustrates the importance of the name one has or is given. There is much thought required in being given a name. Coleman cites Peter Paris' publication *The Spirituality of African Peoples*, in which he emphasizes that within African culture 'proper naming not only acknowledges the child's destiny but also empowers the child to actualize it' (Paris,

1995, pp. 163–4). The naming process may seem irrelevant in Western society, given our discourse, but it is powerful and is so articulated by Lisa Isherwood and Dorothy McEwan in *Introducing Feminist Theology*, where they state, 'the naming process not only expresses and shapes our reality, it also gives us the power to transform our reality' (Isherwood and McEwan, 2001, p. 110). We have acknowledged that projected names disempower Black people, but now we recognize that there is power in naming oneself, which gives Black people the power to transform their reality. If this is true, what do Black people need to do and call themselves as a powerful antidote to negative labelling?

Describing ourselves: what's in a name?

Naming has a history. There is a linkage to the past that signifies and gives meaning to the one who bears the name. What meaning is this? First, it is about Black identity and what it means to the person who is Black. Second, it is the continual assertion of what it means to be Black and created in the image of God. Encompassing both questions, the overarching question is, what does it mean for a Black person created in the image of God to be living in Britain? In this case, despite the negative descriptions placed upon Black life, there is a voice deep within the Black human soul that is rebelling against the imposed restrictive branding and crying out in anguish. These are important existential concerns. But does the Black person define themselves by their colour or by their humanity? To define the black body by its colour is complicated, even for Black people. Researching Black staff experiences in further education, Uvanney Maylor discovered that the term was fluid and problematic (Maylor, 2009). The people having the greatest difficulty in describing themselves as Black were people of South Asian heritage. This example suggests that the term 'Black' cannot be used as a catch-all categorization and throughout the article Maylor highlights the contested nature of the term. I myself made specific reference earlier in this book to 'Black' as those for whom the Middle Passage featured in their cultural history.

Theologically, then, what does it mean to rename yourself? Earlier we explored the importance of the naming process and recognized how naming gives or describes one's identity and destiny. Self-naming must transcend limits of thought and one's imposed reality. This search is a Black person's quest for meaning as they explore who they are. While African history precedes the transatlantic slave trade, the enslavement epoch was a significant disruptive, sending shock waves through the traumatized enslaved. Surely religion must have something to say.

Anthony Pinn, in his book *Terror and Triumph*, posits that at the centre of Black religion is 'complex subjectivity, a desire or a feeling for more life meaning' (Pinn, 2003, p. 173). This is how he conceptualizes the quest:

> In this way, complex subjectivity stands for a healthy self-concept that allows for – even requires – adherence to the privileges and responsibilities associated with those who shape history. It is, then, the creative struggle in history for increased agency, for a fullness of life. Religious experience hence entails a human response to a crisis of identity, and it is the crisis of identity that constitutes the dilemma of ultimacy and meaning … this may be described as a mystical experience, a type of transforming experience that speaks to a deeper reality, guided perhaps by a form of esoteric knowledge. (Pinn, 2003, p. 173)

This self-naming is a deep inner struggle triggered by one's painful external reality. In other words, this self-naming is tantamount to a recreation of self. This self-recreation has been conceptualized by Richard Birt, who writes, 'To become human and develop a human identity is a process of invention (self-invention), of personal and collective action conditioned by social relations' (Birt, 1997, p. 206).

This is introspection that is deep, ongoing and painful, yet remains a continual pursuit of meaning leading to liberation, even if their external realities do not change. However, there is a major problem. In terms of Christianity, many churches, whether Black majority or White majority, seldom take the matter of identity seriously. Most White-led churches see themselves and their theology as normative and the matter of race and identity are seldom considered because 'we are all one in Christ'; meanwhile people on the margins often remain there, even if they attend such churches. For many Black Majority churches, the matter of race is seldom considered and the thought of looking at the biblical text through a Black theological lens is still not well received. Problematically, this deviates from the White theology that many have embraced, where salvation is personal and individualistic and wider concerns are often left to prayer alone because God will sort it all out in due course.

Conclusion

Black people's future lies with themselves. To articulate Black humanity as created in the image of God and assert self-definition will mean empowerment for the marginalized Black self and potentially the destabilizing of the centre of power. Yet, transcending the imposed degradation, Black voices must arise, not to take over but as a human cry and a forceful registering of themselves on White folk's psyche, 'We are here, and will not be silent.'

Not for the self alone, but for all Black people, a new name must be forged and shaped out of the foundry of pain and suffering. There is no need for a literal change of a Eurocentric name to an African name, but rather an awakening Black consciousness of an African past that connects with a collective unconscious that propels many Black people, possibly for the first time in their lives, into an inner place where they are able to appreciate who they are and what their ancestors achieved before Europeans made negative pronouncements on their being. Thus, recreating Black life is not for acceptance, justification or legitimizing by others. It is for acceptance for Black people alone. Vying for acceptance by the other is at present a lost cause and is not worth fighting for. There is no time for fighting for acceptance when so many Black folk have yet to shake off the legacy and consequences of negative labelling.

Joseph Hartopp has summed up the importance of a biblical understanding of names most accurately. He emphasizes its importance in this way:

> Naming is one of the great privileges given to Adam in the Garden of Eden, the power to define the world in certain terms, to label reality and determine people's perceptions of it. To ask what your own name is, is really to ask: 'Who am I?' or indeed: 'Who will I become?' (Hartopp, 2016)

Given names are of fundamental human importance. It is imperative for Black people who have been the victims of negative labelling to create a name and recreate themselves, describing how they understand life as people created in the image of God living in Britain. The name must claim their identity, the place where they accept and love themselves. This name is not for universal acceptance, but is a title enhancing the psychospiritual understanding of their humanity and enabling them to set a pathway to reach their potential. As vital as it is, there is admittedly still a mighty long way to go.

Questions for further reflection

1 Many years ago I worked with a client whose father was a Far-Right Nazi activist. He told me, 'The root of all prejudice is fear.' What do you think?
2 Referring back to Chapter 1, what have you done when you have secretly found yourself discriminating against someone who does not look like you?
3 Where in your life do you feel you need freedom from negatively labelling the other?

Bibliography

Amber, S. (2014), *Malcolm X at Oxford Union: Racial Politics in a Global Era*, Oxford: Oxford University Press.

Asante, M. K. (2003), *Afrocentricity: The Theory of Social Change*, Chicago: African American Images.

Becker, H. (1963), *Outsiders: Studies in the Sociology of Deviance*, New York: A Free Press Paperback.

Beckford, R. (2000), *Dread and Pentecostal: A Political Theology for the Black Church in Britain*, London: Darton, Longman & Todd.

Biko, S. (1978), *Black Consciousness and the Quest for a Humanity*, London: C. Hurst & Co.

Birt, R. (1997), 'Existence, Identity and Liberation', in L. Gordon (ed.), *Existence in Black: An Anthology of Black Existential Philosophy*, New York: Routledge.

Bonnett, A. (2000), *White Identities: Historical and International Perspectives*, Harlow, Essex: Pearson Education Ltd.

Chike, Chigor (2006), 'Black Theology in Britain – One Decade On', *Black Theology: An International Journal*, 4(2), pp. 192–209.

Carmichael, S., https://www.britannica.com/biography/Stokely-Carmichael (accessed 17.3.2021).

Coleman, K. (2007), 'Being Human: A Black British Christian Woman's Perspective', in M. Jagessar and A. Reddie (eds), *Black Theology in Britain: A Reader*, London: Equinox.

Dixon, L. (2000), 'A Reflection on Black Identity and Belonging in the Context of the Anglican Church in England: A Way Forward', *Black Theology in Britain: A Journal of Contextual Practice*, 4, pp. 22–7.

Du Bois, W. (2012), *The Souls of Black Folk*, Oxford: Oxford University Press.

Equality Act (2010), *Diversity Guide – Race/Ethnicity*, https://www.gov.uk/guidance/equality-act-2010-guidance (accessed 15.3.2021).

Fanon, F. (2008), *Black Skin, White Masks*, London: Pluto Press.

Fordham, F. (1966), *An Introduction to Jung's Psychology*, London: Penguin Books.

Garriott, P., Love, K. and Tyler, K. (2008), 'Anti-Black Racism, Self-Esteem, and the Adjustment of White Students in Higher Education', *Journal of Diversity in Higher Education*, 1(1), pp. 45–58.

Garvey, M. (2013), *The Philosophy and Opinions of Marcus Garvey, or Africa for the Africans*, London: Taylor and Francis Group.

Gomez, M. (2005), *Reversing the Sail: A History of the African Diaspora*, New York: Cambridge University Press.

Hartopp, J. (2016), Why Names Are So Important in the Bible – And So Is Yours, https://www.christiantoday.com/article/why-names-are-so-important-in-the-bible-and-so-is-yours/101095.htm (accessed 17.3.2021).

Hill, C. (1958), *Black and White in Harmony: The Drama of West Indians in the Big City, from a London Minister's Notebook*, London: Hodder & Stoughton.

Isherwood, L. and McEwan, D. (2001), *Introducing Feminist Theology*, Sheffield: Sheffield Academic Press.

Isiorho, D. (2002), 'Black Theology in Urban Shadow: Combating Racism in the Church of England', *Black Theology: An International Journal*, 1(1), pp. 29–48.

James, L. R. C. (1984), *80th Birthday Lectures*, London: Race Today.

John, G. (1976), *The New Black Presence in Britain: A Christian Scrutiny*, London: British Council of Churches.

Jung, C. (1974), *Memories, Dreams, Reflections*, London: Random House Inc.

Kaufman, M. (2018), *Black Tudors: The Untold Story*, New York: Simon and Schuster.

Lartey, E. (1999), 'After Stephen Lawrence: Characteristics and Agenda for Black Theology in Britain', *Black Theology in Britain: A Journal of Contextual Praxis*, 3, pp. 79–91.

Marley, R. (1980), 'Redemption Song', *Uprising*, Jamaica: Tuff Gong Island.

Maylor, U. (2009), 'What Is the Meaning of "Black"? Researching "Black" Respondents', *Ethnic and Racial Studies*, 32(2), pp. 369–87.

Paris, P. (1995), *The Spirituality of African Peoples: The Search for a Common Moral Discourse*, Minneapolis: Augsburg Fortress.

Perkinson, J. (2004), *White Theology: Outing Supremacy in Modernity*, New York: Palgrave Macmillan.

Pinn, A. B. (2003), *Terror and Triumph: The Nature of Black Religion*, Minneapolis: Augsburg Fortress.

Rajiv, S. (1992), *Forms of Black Consciousness*, New York: Stosius Inc/ Advent Books Division.

Reddie, A. (2006), *Black Theology in Transatlantic Dialogue*, New York: Palgrave Macmillan.

Smith, R. (2007), *Youth Justice: Ideas, Policy and Practice*, Cullompton, Devon: Willan Publishing.

Sturge, M. (2005), *Look What the Lord Has Done: An Exploration of Black Christian Faith in Britain*, Bletchley: Scripture Union.

Van Der Kolk, B. A. (2014), *The Body Keeps the Score: Mind, brain, and body in the healing of trauma*, London: Penguin Books.

Williams, C. (1987), *The Destruction of Black Civilization: Great Issues of a Race From 4500 B.C. to 2000 A.D.*, Chicago: Third World Press.

6

Towards a Theology of Black Men and Radical Self-Love in the UK: Beyond the Exotic and the Grotesque

The children, having seen the spectacular defeat of their fathers – having seen what happens to any bad nigger and, still more, what happens to the good ones – cannot listen to their fathers and certainly will not listen to the society which is responsible for their orphaned condition. (James Baldwin, 1966, 'A Report from Occupied Territory')

Poverty creates conditions that make young, uneducated and unemployed Black [men] into scavengers. They are forced to live or die by chance. It is this peculiar reality where criminality, the denial of work, poverty, and Black maleness puts Black men and boys toward the prison and ultimately toward death at the hands of the police or other Black [men] forced to scavenge for survival ... This class bias from which Black people generally, but Black [men] particularly, are observed is saturated with condemnation, not earnestness or understanding. (Tommy J. Curry, 2017, *The Man-Not: Race, Class, Genre, and the Dilemmas of Black Manhood*)

Introduction

Long given to racial delusions about their origins (MacDougall, 1982) and genetic purity (Poliakov, 1974), English White men have imposed on the Black man presumed danger, devilishness and moral otherworldliness. Strikingly, the Black man has also been a desired object: the homosocial, homosexual and evil doppelganger to the 'civilized' Englishman. He is desired as much as despised, which is how he is conjured in the White man's (and woman's) imagination. In the sixteenth century, the Tudors and Stuarts heard about Black men through lore and mythical exclamations from the pulpit about black devils, and everyday speech about blackamoors was used to scare children into obedience. They were a common sight in the royal court, the homes of the nobility, London and its nearby towns and beyond (Kauffman, 2017; Onyeka, 2013; Wood, 2012). Elizabeth I, an investor in Sir John Hawkins' slave-raiding ventures, sought to expel Africans from London, and from England. Five hundred years before Enoch Powell's infamous 'rivers of blood' speech, Elizabeth I wrote in an open letter in 1596 to various political dignitaries. 'Her Majesty, understanding that several blackamoors have lately been brought into this realm, of which kind there are already too many here ... her Majesty's pleasure therefore is that those kind of people should be expelled from the land' (quoted Fryer, 1984, pp. 10–11).

Alarmed by the large Black population, an exasperated Elizabeth, being 'highly discontented', hired a German slave dealer to abduct Black people and sell them into Caribbean slavery (Linebaugh and Rediker, 2013). Shakespeare's plays, displaying his own anti-Black racism, electrified commoner and noble alike with sordid hypersexual tales, priapic potential rapists and savage Black men, who threatened violence and racial degradation through forced miscegenation (Jordan, 1977; Lyons, 1975).

History, as noted by James Baldwin (1990), Frantz Fanon (1967), John Henrik Clarke (1974), Malcolm X (1970), and Carter G. Woodson (2009), shows the Black man living in an uncompromising space where literally and symbolically he battles on the White man's terms. He is a metaphorical prisoner to the White man's ontological, psychosexual expressions, self-conscious anxieties and insecurities, through their patriarchal cultural complexes demonizing the other. As John Henrik Clarke notes, 'Black people must always remember that Western civilization was not created with them in mind' (Henrik Clarke, 1974). Fanon explains this dilemma:

From within the metaphor of vision complicit with a Western metaphysic of Man emerges the displacement of the colonial relation. The Black presence ruins the representative narrative of Western personhood: its past tethered to treacherous stereotypes of primitivism and degeneracy will not produce a history of civil progress, a space for the socius; its presence, dismembered and dislocated, will not contain the image of identity that is questioned in the dialectic of the mind/body and resolved in the epistemology of 'appearance and reality.' The White man's eyes break up the Black man's body and in that act of epistemic violence its own frame of reference is transgressed, its field of vision disturbed. (Fanon, 1986, p. xii)

Fanon's comments underline the understanding that both the oppressed and the oppressor need liberating.

As a Black Christian minister and counsellor, born and socialized in Britain, I have seen British racism cause havoc in Black men's lives and it is proper that I should contemplate the need of Black men for radical self-love.

I understand Christian ministry as a site for resistance to anti-Black racism and a force that uplifts the Black man from the pernicious and long-standing psychosexual anxieties and projections that view him as a grotesque stain on the 'Anglo-Saxon' nation. The Black man, his family and community face a dire situation in Britain. While advocates struggle to effect change in policies and the state makes efforts to make and enforce laws, the Black man's existence and spiritual life is being ignored. Moreover, formal equality cannot dismiss embedded contempt, denigration and negation without a corresponding need for his material and psychospiritual renewal. The White man must look within to discover love in himself without finding his worth by dehumanizing others. This is not my or any other Black man's concern. As Marcus Garvey exclaimed, 'Hear all, but attend only to that which concerns you' (Garvey, 1986, p. 320), for in reality the Black man, being objectified for five hundred years, cannot expect assistance from his oppressor nor imagine him as his equal.

My concern is addressing the two central questions posited by Frantz Fanon's *Black Skin, White Masks*: first, 'What does a man want?' and second, 'What does the Black man want?' (Fanon, 1986, p. 10). The questions lead me to ask, what does the Black man *mean* to himself in a White world that denies his humanity? With such a tortured ontology, Ta-Nehisi Coates, like other writers, insists that the Black man must make a world for himself. Coates writes: 'This is your country, this is your world, this is your body, and you must find some way to live within the all of it' (Coates, 2015, p. 12).

The historical context has been laid and I want to explore three major themes. First, the Black male's social determinants, highlighting discrimination faced in health, employment, education and social wellbeing within the UK including the dichotomy of how the Black male is potentially viewed as both exotic and grotesque. Second, the Black man's innate desire for self-love within a dangerous context. Here, self-love must not be confused with narcissism. Third, understanding the Black man's desire for self-love through a Black theological lens, concentrating on Christianity's historical African centredness; thus the Black man can draw from this rich history to develop self-love. This chapter serves as a meditation on how the Black man can live and learn to re-love himself. In addition, given the brutal murder of George Floyd by the police in the USA and the global backlash of this act, Black men are highlighted as they still appear to be targets for violence and continual injustice.

Social determinants of health and anti-Black misandry in the UK

The anti-Black Elizabethan histories described earlier resonate today, manifesting themselves in measurable ways. In patriarchal societies, it is axiomatic, especially where state policies are favourable to intergenerational inequity and wealth transfers, and children's social attainments are strongly correlated to their father's social status. This was admitted in the USA by

Senator Daniel Moynihan's infamous 1965 report, *The Negro Family: The Case for National Action*, commonly known as the Moynihan Report. Senator Moynihan blamed the Black family's problem on single-parent mother households and absentee fathers and not government policies and anti-Black racism in the corporate sector and civil society.

Fifty years on from Moynihan's report in America, the Black man in the UK – particularly the African Caribbean man – is in trouble. Unemployment in Britain in 2018 was 4 per cent, translating to 6.3 per cent among African Caribbean men and 3.6 per cent among White men. By contrast, during the 2008 global financial crash, unemployment for those from White backgrounds averaged around 7.8 per cent, but around 14.7 per cent for people from the Black and Asian minority ethnic groups (Foley, 2020). In 2020, during the coronavirus pandemic, unemployment in the UK was 5 per cent overall: 4.5 per cent in White populations, and 8.5 per cent for marginalized populations. Nor could the rate of deaths within such communities be ignored by the British government or society. Unpublished government statistics provide a bleak picture for young Black men: 'Unemployment among young Black men has doubled in three years, rising from 28.8 per cent in 2008 to 55.9 per cent in the last three months of 2011' (Ball et al., 2012). Admittedly, unemployment in the UK is highest among Pakistani and Bangladeshi communities, but there are other issues than unemployment. For example, African and Caribbean Britons' experience of criminal justice is high and there is an over-representation of mental health crises. The British population comprises approximately 3 per cent of Black men and boys making up around 50 per cent of mental illness. While mental illness among minority groups is a complex matter, 'a black man in the UK is seventeen times more likely than a white man to be diagnosed with a serious mental health condition such as schizophrenia or bipolar. Black people are also four times more likely to be sectioned under the Mental Health Act' (Fanin, 2017, para. 12).

(Un)employment and mental health challenges culminate in the racism found within the UK criminal justice system.

Hayden Smith (2017) notes that, according to a Ministry of Justice report, nine out of 10,000 Black Britons spend time in youth custody compared to one White youth in 10,000. Smith's commentary emphasizes that while there has been a substantial decrease in custody across all ethnicities, such decrease for BAME groups has been slower; thus the custodial rates for BAME communities have increased proportionately over the last decade. Adding to this troubling picture, the arrest rate for young Black men is three times higher than for their White counterparts. This situation is worsened when we recognize that, relative to White youth, Black youth serve longer periods in custody with longer 'sentence lengths for violence against the person, theft and possession of weapons' (Smith, 2017, para. 12). Given these facts, the myths surrounding Black men as a dangerous threat to White people's wellbeing are still prevalent.

That Black men are seen as threats and dangerous, in need of controlling and surveillance, is, as Dorothy Roberts records in *Fatal Invention*, evidenced by 'The disproportionate storage of their genetic profiles in state and federal databases', such as Scotland Yard (Roberts, 2011, p. 277). Roberts reports that 41 per cent of African Americans are registered in the Combined DNA Index System (CODIS); in the UK, 40 per cent of all Black men and 77 per cent of all young Black men (aged 15 to 35) have their genetic profiles stored in the Scotland Yard's DNA database. By comparison, only 6 per cent of White men have DNA stored in the UK. This genetic encircling contributes to the criminalization of Black men and boys in the UK, marking them off for genocidal possibilities.

Because employment and financial security increase people's access to resources aiding their wellbeing, family and community, it is also important, in analysing this dilemma, to review employment – and, specifically, remuneration – statistics for Black men compared with their White colleagues.

As Rianna Croxford summarizes, the Russell Group revealed that in the UK, 'black and Arab academics at the UK's top universities earn an average 26 percent less than white colleagues and female academics fare even worse, with an ethnicity pay gap on top of the gender pay gap' (Croxford, 2018, para. 9). Other studies, including St George's University Hospital's (2018) report for the National Health Service (NHS), demonstrate that there is an increasing income gap between BAME workers compared to their White counterparts doing similar work (Therrin, 2018). Given these two great institutions in the UK, one dare not imagine what might be occurring in other industries with BAME employees.

There are two final notes on racial pay gaps worth mentioning. First, the Human Rights and Equality Commission's Report (2018) concludes that pay was determined by several factors including whether someone was born abroad or in the UK. The implication is that 'language and cultural barriers, confronted by immigrants, had an effect on pay' (Longhi and Brynin, 2017). Furthermore, Black African and Black Caribbean male employees, whether born overseas or in the UK, when compared to their White colleagues, 'experience[d] a pay gap', anywhere from 3.5 per cent to over 6.4 per cent (Longhi and Brynin, 2017). Second, ethnic or migrant workers reported that they experienced higher stress levels in their daily lives. Discrimination and its stressful consequences in the workplace require more research (Giga et al., 2008).

The foregoing crises experienced by Black men in the UK mire them in a struggle for survival and a scramble to capitalize on loosely fallen crumbs from trickle-down remnants from the UK's elites. These crises are, in concrete terms, attributable to Thatcherite neoliberal policies which have been continued by successive Conservative and Labour regimes. The present crisis is endemic in the UK; it is economic and predicated on exclusionary government policies resulting from ingrained attitudes and discriminatory racist practices within British society. Stuart Hall and Bill Schwarz (2017) and Paul Gilroy (2002/2013) notably located the contemporary branches of British racism in Britain's colonial afterlife: policing, media practices and political culture. For example, the Conservative Party, led by David Cameron and subsequently by Theresa May, sought to 'transport' Jamaican criminal offenders back to Jamaica. Those lively to history cannot help but notice that this political behaviour is far from new. English governments have often scapegoated onto 'their' colonies those marginalized by public policies at home. For example, Cromwell and his ilk (and subsequent administrations) transported Irish religious heretics, criminal offenders, sex workers, vagrants and other assorted undesirables to American and Caribbean colonies throughout the eighteenth century, and to Australia and South Africa in the nineteenth century. Adding insult to indignity, the Windrush generation, now in their twilight years, are threatened with deportation after making significant contributions to the UK.

British racism, and its effects which Black men heroically struggle to transcend, is not limited to that generation; it extends to their families and their unborn children. What is helping us to understand intergenerational trauma and its effects on relationships, the body, family and the social environment is epigenetics.

There is insufficient space in this chapter to explore epigenetics in detail, but new insights are helping us to understand and appreciate human complexity, especially what happens when people encounter life-threatening and traumatic experiences. Epigenetics explains how genes are read by cells and, subsequently, how these readings produce particular proteins. Epigenetics shows that existential and ontological traumas (such as those experienced through racial violence) impact parents, adults and their offspring. What has been felt by the offspring from those previously traumatized is as though they experienced the trauma firsthand. These epigenetic impacts may contribute to poor social outcomes compounded by problematic responses to irrational social conditions. Teen Vogue journalist Lincoln Anthony Blades outlines this interplay between epigenetics and intergenerational trauma. He states that '[i]f the Holocaust caused immense human disruption, intense enough to cause trauma to survivors, the abject horrors and brutality suffered by the enslaved is likely to have similar effects on black slavery descendants worldwide' (Blades, 2016, para. 5).

Blades builds on psychiatrist Dr Rachel Yehuda's pioneering work on epigenetics. Examining trauma from a psychiatric and neuroscientific perspective, Yehuda piloted a small group comprising her neighbours who had survived the Jewish Holocaust. She found that the Holocaust survivors had a similar hormonal profile to Vietnam veterans suffering from PTSD. Years later, studying Holocaust survivors' offspring, Yehuda discovered the following: 'Holocaust offspring had the same neuroendocrine or hormonal abnormalities that we were viewing in Holocaust survivors and persons with post-traumatic stress disorder' (Yehuda, 2015, para. 44). In a later study, psychiatrist John Krystal states, '[t]he observation that the same genes might be affected in parents and children suggests something specific, perhaps related to stress response, is being conveyed from parent to child' (Krystal, 2016, para. 11). Survivors from remote historical traumas having similar physiological traces in the present is odd but worth investigating. Yehuda's and Krystal's research confirms earlier psychosocial conceptualizations articulated by social scientist Joy DeGruy in *Post Traumatic Slave Syndrome*. DeGruy asks, 'Isn't it likely that many slaves were severely traumatized? Furthermore, did the trauma and the effects of such horrific abuse end with the abolition of slavery?' (DeGruy, 2005, cover copy). As argued by James H. Sweet (2003), routinized starvation, amputations, rapes (of men and women), and brutal work regimes from the cradle to the grave severely marked each enslaved African. Sweet writes:

> As ... young slaves grew into mature adults, they reacted to their childhood traumas in a variety of ways. Some were most certainly broken by the accumulation of suffering that they were forced to endure. We can never be sure about the rate of psychological disorder among slaves, but it must have been high. Notations of 'crazy' (*louco/a*) slaves in property inventories are not unusual. (Sweet, 2003, p. 81)

Enslavement's brutality, capturing and torturing bodies, enslaving Black minds and disrupting one's culture in the Caribbean, was followed by Jim Crow and lynching in the USA, so no end there to the dehumanizing of black bodies. Since then enslavement, objectification and violence have been normalized. Bear in mind that it was not long ago that many Caribbean islands won independence from their colonizers, or the 1960s Civil Rights had victories in the USA. Nation building, developing an infrastructure to address the severe traumas Black people experienced and have passed along to subsequent generations is a recent phenomenon.

The exotic and the grotesque

From a psychosocial perspective, the Black man's current situation in the West has its roots in the White man's imagination, where he is portrayed as both exotic and grotesque. Anti-Black racism and antipathy towards Black men has deep historical roots. Going back to the fifteenth century there was an ambivalent mix of desire and exoticization, along with the imagined repulsion towards Black men. All around us there are associations with Black men and boys' presumed hypersexuality and sexual misconduct running deep within English culture. In *To Wash an Aethiopian White*, Charles Lyons records Eurocentric ideology dismissing Black people from being equals. This history reinforces the notion that perceiving the black body in a negative light has its origins, in part, in the Elizabethan period. Lyons comments, 'In Elizabethan poetry, drama, and common speech of the day, the black man was generally referred to as a lecher, a degenerate, a devil, an animal' (Lyons, 1975, p. 1). When British travellers arrived in Africa, they transported and projected these beliefs – which were already entrenched in their conscious and unconscious minds – onto the unsuspecting African. As is commonly known, ideas carry, and what is *believed* to be real is *taken as* real. During the time of the Tudors and the Stuarts, the racial fantasies and ideologies, reinforced by scientific mores, that Black people are biologically and psychologically inferior and insensible to pain and suffering had taken deep root (Lyons, 1975).

The exotic

The *exotic* carries its own intricacies and examining its etymology matters. At its most primal, the word means 'belonging to another country, foreign' (*Oxford English Dictionary*, n.d.). Demonstrating its complexity, English professor Graham Huggan emphasizes that '[w]e need to revisit the history of exoticist representation and trace exoticism's development from a privileged mode of aesthetic symbol to its contemporary status as a global mode of mass consumption' (Huggan, 2001, p. 13). He further writes that

> exotic is not, as is often supposed, an inherent *quality* to be found 'in' certain people, distinctive objects, or specific places; exotic describes, rather, a particular mode of aesthetic perception – one which renders people, objects and places strange even as it tries to domesticate them, and which effectively manufactures otherness even as it claims to surrender to its immanent mystery. (Huggan, 2001, p. 13)

The exotic is something that is other, odd and different. In other words, the person who observes the exotic Other simultaneously sees them as beautiful and attempts to dominate them.

Similarly, Professor of Comparative Religion Dorothy Matilda Figueira argues that the exotic has a 'foreignness' tinge. She advances the concept that the 'exotic has a special force which can be strangely beautiful and unfamiliarly enticing. This physical and (meta) physical identification at the heart of the exotic accounts for the tension it often presents between extraneity and the erotic' (Figueira, 1994, p. 1). Huggan's and Figueira's interpretations depict the exotic as a mystical-like and desirable quality difficult to describe and unquantifiable.

The cultural scholar Ronald Jackson offers another description. He conceptualizes the Black male body as problematic by being visible and peripheral. In defining the African American Black man's body, Jackson concludes, the 'Black [man's] body is exotic and strange, violent, incompetent and uneducated, sexual, exploitable and innately incapacitated' (Jackson, 2006, p. 75). A similar understanding is articulated by professor of communication Maurice Hall. Hall challenges the alleged Black man's low status and asserts that Jamaica and the Caribbean have produced world leaders in various disciplines. He admits, 'there are still enduring Western caricatures of the Caribbean male as breezily self-assertive, yet devoid of substance, exotic, and anti-intellectual' (Hall, 2011, p. 35).

James Baldwin derided the term 'exotic' in his 'Stranger in the Village'. Being a visitor in a Swiss village that had never seen a Black man walk through their streets, Baldwin, at times filled with rage and astonishment at his apparent oddity for the locals, writes: 'The black man insists, by whatever means he finds at his disposal, that the white man cease to regard him as an exotic rarity and recognize him as a human being' (Baldwin, 1955, p. 8).

The point is that the Black man, exoticized and grotesque and produced and reproduced in the psychosexual reality of the White collective imagination, has real consequences for both the White 'subject' and the Black 'object'. Such tropes shield the White self from the moral responsibility for (a) being passively obfuscating and refusing to acknowledge the Black man's humanity (that is, implicit bias); and (b) actively and rationally securing White self-interests by discriminating against the Black man through physical violence (e.g., Stephen Lawrence's murder), degradation (i.e., dehumanization), and social exclusion (e.g., imprisonment and unemployment).

From a feminist perspective, Rachel Kuo problematizes the exotic. Kuo argues that although there may be good intentions in calling a dark-skinned woman 'exotic', what White men are doing is giving us dark-skinned people a backhanded 'reminder that in a white society, we are less normal, less human, and less real than white people' (Kuo, 2015, sect. 5, para. 1). Kuo's later analysis stresses that '[b]eing called exotic is rooted and entrenched in violence. On the surface, it seems compliment-ary, and at worse, a casual faux pas, the historical and current impact of exotifying women of color has targeted us for sexual violence' (Kuo, 2016, sect. 4, para. 6). For the ones describing them this mystique and sensual definition directed at such women dehumanizes them as Others. The notion of the exotic thus leads to its antagonistic bedfellow: the grotesque.

The grotesque

Being labelled as grotesque is complicated and demeaning. The term means '[c]haracterized by distortion or unnatural combinations; fantastically extravagant; bizarre' as well as 'fantastically absurd' (*Oxford English Dictionary*). Professor of English and American Literature Leonard Cassuto asserts that '[h]uman objectification can result from multiple perceived differences, but in [white] American culture it happens most readily to people with dark skin' (Cassuto, 1996, p. 3). Cassuto illustrates that 'racial objectification was institutionalized by slavery, but (as the colonial experience demonstrates) it has never been limited to that practice' (p. 3).

With this ambivalent lived experience of exotic and grotesque, the Black man finds himself in a difficult position. Frantz Fanon refers to this existential dilemma:

> The black man has no ontological resistance in the eyes of the white man. Overnight the Negro has been given two frames of reference within which he has had to place himself. His metaphysics, or, less pretentiously, his customs and the sources on which they were based, were wiped out because they were in conflict with a civilization that he did not know and that imposed itself on him. (Fanon, 1986, p. 110)

Fanon theorizes that, on the one hand, from the oppressor's viewpoint, the Black man is unimportant and therefore can be erased from Western history. In one sense, he no longer exists, but has been given another existence, an anaemic former self. He is now the Western bogeyman, another scapegoat who has been given ill-fitting, unkempt clothes to hide him. On the other hand, this erasure requires recognition that the Black man is a large, absent *presence*. While the Black man's body is seen as grotesque, Fanon suggests that, in reality, this perception is a process reactive formation in which the Black-man-as-grotesque is an unconscious White male projection, similar to a cathartic releasing of primal repression and suppression in which the Black man's body is appropriated as the convenient receptacle for the White man's fractious inner psychic machinations. The White man, in short, becomes whole through fantasy projections onto the Black man who, mysteriously and without any effort or physiological change, is morphed into another being occupying an imposed exotic and grotesque identity.

From these descriptions, the Black man's plight is a harrowing existence, filled with complications and contradictions many of which he has unwittingly consumed, much to his demise. Underpinning the terms *Blackness*, *exotic*, and *grotesque* is a deep-seated repulsion mainly by the White male other. This repulsive fear views and treats the Black man with hatred that mirrors its other: desire. I would be remiss to ignore how influential the Black male body has been, albeit through a Black religious lens, described by professor of religion Anthony Pinn (2003). Pinn's contribution is based in the American context, but it has applicability throughout the diaspora. His comments are noteworthy:

> I am just as interested in the body lived as I am in the body as metaphor. Therefore, I am not suggesting that experience is simple physiological data: rather, I understand the body as complex. Because of this, I make no attempt to talk in terms of the body as a universal symbol or representing a universally lived history. Hence, the body may mean something different in each cultural and historical context. (Pinn, 2003, p. 236)

Pinn's assertion bucks the notion that the Black male experience is homogenous. Each location of oppression will have nuanced expression by those living within it. Although I am presenting a general picture about living in a Black male body, it is crucial to keep subjective experience at the forefront of one's mind.

Using a Fanonist psychosocial history to describe Black men in the UK, and having explored their paradoxical location as both exotic and grotesque, I now turn to theorizing the psychological imposition on those that bear such burdens. I aim to develop a radical self-love for the Black man in becoming an intentional resilient person that uplifts his own humanity.

Black men and the struggle for survival

Self-actualization for the Black man is reflected in Bob Marley's 1980 classic 'Redemption Song'. He makes it clear that it is the Black man's task to free himself from mental slavery, because only he can liberate his own mind (Marley, 1980). Using Black theology as a lens for analysis, Marley's lyrics are a 'theology of survival', that 'refuses to accept conditions as they are' nor to accept conditions as 'being the will of God'. Furthermore, James Cone, the godfather of Black theology, fiercely contends that Black people must strive 'to make sense of their existence in a white society whose suffering and humiliation is beyond rational explanation' (Cone, 2020, p. 17).

Self-love is difficult within an environment where one struggles for survival, but survival and thriving is the Black man's responsibility as he reworks his psychosocial position. If one takes the Black man's history seriously, one wonders how he has survived, given the continual effort expended for his annihilation. The African American clinical psychologist Naim Akbar explores this matter of survival in *Visions for Black Men*. Akbar states, 'Given all the odds; given the almost impossible circumstances we have faced; given these barriers which would have devastated any other human breed a long time ago – the simple question is: Why are we still here anyway?' (Akbar, 1992, back cover).

Given the relentless brutality that Black men have endured, one must assume that they are seen in the perpetrators' eyes as being 'nonhuman' (Curry, 2017). Curry's descriptions make for frighteningly dismal reading. He writes:

Popular categories of analysis such as class, gender, and even race suppose a universal human template upon which they imprint. But what is the applicability of human categories on the nonhuman? The black male is negated not from an origin (human) being, but from nihility ... [N]onbeing expresses the condition of black male being – the nihility from which he is birthed. (Curry, 2017, p. 6)

From Curry's position, the Black man is hard to categorize; from earlier cited descriptions, the Black man, his imposed construction and distorted labelling highlights the fact that he alone must create a life for himself, a life worth living. He has no other alternative but to remove his mental shackles imposed by a foreign imagination and forge a lived understanding pertaining to self-love and self-image that requires neither acceptance nor validation from any White person. This self-sculpting is a painful, lifelong endeavour transcending any ready-made packages relating to self-love purchased in local bookstores or online shops. For me, a biblical narrative provides a milieu for a self-love emerging from a place of authenticity.

Towards self-love: creating a life worth living

To give some context to an understanding in helping Black men, I will draw on some generalizations from scenarios in which I have been involved.

Given my role as a minister and community leader, I have, on many occasions, been asked by families to officiate at funerals for their loved ones who have taken their own lives. It is an honour being asked to undertake such a service at a most sensitive and painful time in their lives.

All the men whose funerals I have officiated at were jovial and sociable, but they, like us, carried a darker side, struggling with life and their mental wellbeing. Many had similar early life experiences. First, many were raised by a single parent and were either unsure of who their father was or had never met him. Secondly, many had not learnt to talk about their emotions, thus suppressing their pain, especially during troubling times, leading to violent expressive episodes. Third, many used alcohol or other drugs to self-medicate against excruciating existential pain.

How is it possible for Black men to begin the healing process? I suggest it is possible by turning to a biblical text in developing a way to deal with Black men's plight. It can be found in Jesus' encounter with the Pharisees and Sadducees who questioned him on many issues, to which he responds through parables. A scribe – one who copies ancient religious text – overhearing Jesus' condemning comments about the temple administrators, challenges him by asking, 'Which is the first commandment of all?' (Mark 12.28, New King James Version). And Jesus answers him:

[T]he first of all the commandments is, Hear, O Israel; The Lord our God is one Lord: And thou shalt love the Lord thy God with all thy heart, and with all thy soul, and with all thy mind, and with all thy strength: this is the first commandment. And the second is like, namely this, Thou shalt love thy neighbour as thyself. There is none other commandment greater than these. (Mark 12.29–31, King James Version)

Jesus' teachings were uttered during a time of Roman global expansion, imperialism and violence, coupled with the oppression of the Jewish people and imposing how they practised their faith. The Black man has existed in a context of global expansion, imperialism and violence and must somehow transcend his current situation if he is going to have a worthy existence now and in the future – that is, an existence in which he does not continually find himself the underdog while the West continues to flex its muscles as it displays an insatiable thirst for world domination.

Arguably, even if a Black man has risen far in his profession today, he can still be perceived as the stooge. George Yancy explores this notion in his article 'The Ugly Truth about Being a Black Professor in America' (2018), highlighting the continual racial incongruence in which he lives. For example, in recent years racial tensions have increased globally, in 2020 with the Black Lives Matter protests and demonstrations, but beginning in more recent times with the rants by the former American President Donald Trump; Marine Le Pen, the French far-right leader; other right wing groups in Europe; Brexit in the UK; and the recent results from a long-term study within the UK National Health Service exposing the fact that BAME groups are paid less than their peers for doing the same work (Campbell, 2018).

Returning to Jesus' comments, the scribe asks one question but Jesus challenges him further. As a practising clergyman, and someone who has spent many years involved in church life, I have heard countless sermons on loving God and many sermons on loving one's neighbour. To this date, as a mature man, I have never heard a sermon on self-love, ever. One cannot ignore that the root of much of the existential angst experienced by Black men is self-loathing and its destructive effect on the psyche, which often finds its outlet in harm to themselves and others.

Self-love versus narcissism

Psychologists use the terms self-love, self-care and self-compassion interchangeably. It is important to make a distinction between the self-love taught by Jesus and narcissistic love that focuses totally on self-centredness. The self-love taught by Jesus is love that treats oneself healthily and manifests itself in helping others, leading to healthy self-understanding and relationship with God. Another definition is, 'Self-love is not simply a state of feeling good. It is a state of appreciation for oneself that *grows from actions* that support our physical, psychological and spiritual growth. Self-love is dynamic; it grows through actions that mature us' (Khoshaba, 2012, para. 4). In other words, we are able to accept our total selves.

Given their plight, many Black men have not learnt to appreciate themselves in a meaningful way in order to cope with life's problems. It must be stressed that appreciating yourself with loving action includes contemplation, doing fulfilling labour, eating healthily, exercising, reading, wearing good clothes, and looking good. It is this, and more. It is a constant assessing, reassessing and, with equanimity, forgiving oneself, and forgiving and living in peace with others.

The Black man learning to love himself is more than a three-step plan. It often begins with pain in acknowledging one's Blackness, and continues on an internal excursion, deconstructing and reconstructing in communion with like-minded sojourners; we are, after all, the company we keep. One way for Black men to begin this is to rediscover their Black selfhood by finding an appropriate person to talk with as a means of self-exploration. One of the crises of masculinity is that men seldom talk about their emotional life. In other words, all men, but Black men in particular, need, quite literally, to learn a new language and vocabulary that will enable them to explore their hearts, minds and souls. To the Black men reading this: pay a professional, if necessary, to assist in discovering who you are and to assist you in finding your purpose, place and God-given potential. The epigram over Egyptian temples was, 'Man, Know Thyself!'

It is ironic that something as crucial as knowing yourself is not invested in, but often given lip service while spending lavishly on consumer products that reduce in value and fade with age (Burrell, 2010). For example, many spend thousands on expensive cars but baulk at spending a few hundred pounds or dollars to help themselves become better human beings. This represents a consumption-driven social order prioritizing fleeting material goods.

Reclaiming history as a portal for loving the self

Another way to learn self-love is to combat the self-loathing common in the Black man, especially those born in the West. The challenge is to discover facts about African people and recognize their achievements prior to the European onslaught and before conscious attempts were made to obliterate the

African past from those to whom it would matter most – Black people (see Clarke, 1974; Malcolm X, 1970; Woodson, 2009).

You may wonder what history has to do with self-love. To understand this, we need to understand how vital history is for people who have been told they have no history and have made little or no contribution to the planet. Reclaiming history can, for the Black man, demonstrate the vitality and strength his ancestors possessed as a people. John Henrik Clarke (1974), quoted in Dr Lumumba Umunna Ubani's *Afrikan Mind Reconnection and Spiritual Re-Awakening*, endorses history's importance, asserting that

> [h]istory is not everything, but it is a starting point. History is a clock that people use to tell their political and cultural time of day. It is a compass they use to find themselves on the map of human geography. It tells them where they are but, more importantly, what they must be. (Ubani, 2011, p. 405)

Knowing one's history is pivotal in gaining self-respect, self-love, and reinforces how belonging is important.

Radical self-love for the Black man cannot wait. It does not require validation, approval, or legitimization from White people. There is little in the Western social fabric that reflects positive Black men other than images that are often disturbing to his wellbeing and existence. Black men have learnt, and have been conditioned, not to love themselves. However, what is learnt can be unlearnt with guidance, education, support and a willingness to change while making allies with like-minded communities.

The Bible and human freedom

Undeniably, the Bible has been used as an oppressive tool and is, for some Black people, problematic. Yet the Bible has also been used to bring liberation. Indeed, resistance to slavery is, in some cases, directly linked to biblical discourses. However, Susan Buck-Morss contends that there was an African Muslim minority enslaved in the Americas, one being Boukman (i.e., 'Book Man', so named because he was literate), who was enslaved in Jamaica before being sold into slavery in Haiti and is considered the spiritual founder of the Haitian Revolution (Buck-Morss, 2009). Caribbean diaspora theologian Delroy Reid-Salmon (2012) contests this idea and cogently argues that the 1831 Jamaican Baptist War was led by Baptist deacon Sam Sharpe, who using the Bible mobilized the enslaved to confront slavery. Garnett Roper (2015) argues a similar point when he states that Sharpe was most influenced by his religious faith, which was assisted by his reading of the Jewish and Christian scriptures. (See my earlier comment in Chapter 3.)

Similarly, on American soil, Howard Thurman, African American author, philosopher, theologian, educator and civil rights leader, writes:

> The basic fact is that Christianity as it was born in the mind of this Jewish teacher and thinker [Jesus] appears as a technique of survival of the oppressed. That it became, through the intervening years, a religion of the powerful and the dominant, sometimes used as an instrument of oppression, must not tempt us into believing it was thus in the mind of Jesus. 'In Him was life, and the life was the light of men.' Wherever his spirit appears, the oppressed gather fresh courage; for he announced the good news that fear, hypocrisy and hatred, the three hounds of hell that tracked the trail of the disinherited, need have no dominion over them. (Thurman, 1996, p. 29)

Thurman argues that Jesus' agenda was never for entrapping or exploiting people. Again from the Caribbean context, William David Spencer in *Dread Jesus* quotes a well-known saying by Marcus Garvey, the Jamaican political activist and philosopher:

> I believe in God the Father, God the Son, and God the Holy Spirit. I endorse the Nicene Creed. I believe that Jesus died for me. I believe that God lives for me as for all men, and

no condition you can impose upon me by deceiving me about Christianity will cause me to doubt Jesus Christ and to doubt God. I shall never hold Christ responsible for the commercialization of Christianity by the heartless men who adopt it as the easiest means of fooling and robbing other people out of their land and country. (Spencer, 1998, p. 134)

Marcus Garvey was resolute in Christianity's true nature and recognized that his own work, human liberation, was in keeping with Jesus' agenda.

The African theologian John Mbiti (1990) stresses that Christianity had deep African roots going back many centuries. It is worthwhile to recall the Ethiopian eunuch who, travelling home to Ethiopia from Jerusalem, met Philip, a Jesus follower. The nameless yet eminent Ethiopian, reading the scriptures and recognizing their value, does not understand what he is reading. When he meets Philip, they enter into a conversation concerning the scriptures and, having the text explained, he accepts the message and asks to be baptized. After his baptism, the Bible states that Philip continued his unknown mission and the eunuch returned home rejoicing (Acts 8.32, New King James Version).

The unfolding story has the eunuch returning home and sharing the great news he experienced (Cole-Rous, n.d.). Later in history, Christianity had an influence on the city of Alexandria in Egypt (Griggs, 1990). Christianity has had a long and enduring history in Africa and in Black people's lives. Indeed, Egypt was where the infant Jesus was sent for protection against the infanticidal Herod; North Africa (Numidia) was where St Augustine was born, raised and converted, and where many 'Church Fathers' sought isolation and contemplation. Moreover, in the Old Testament, Egypt was where Abram sojourned before being renamed Abraham; where Joseph rose to high status in Pharaoh's household; and where Moses, like Osiris before him, was saved by a maidservant from drowning in the Nile. According to John Mbiti, Christianity became problematic in Africa during the eighteenth century when European missionaries arrived who, in sharing the gospel, thought they were bringing something new to Africa. The Christian faith had been alive in Africa long before the arrival of European or American missionaries. On this matter, Mbiti emphasizes:

> For Africans, the whole existence is a religious phenomenon; man is a deeply religious being living in a religious universe. Failure to realize and understand this starting point, has led missionaries, anthropologists, colonial administrators, and other foreign writers on African religions to misunderstand not only the religions as such but the peoples of Africa. (Mbiti, 2015, p. 15).

From these examples, it is evident that the Christian faith has been central in African sensibility and was a significant life force. Thus, in relation to the biblical narrative, crypto-Islam and subsequent Islamic conversions, the Bible was, during slavery, used as a code for ensuring the Black man's survival in the West. I now turn to the biblical text – taken as either a religious or secular meditation on self-love – to create a way of dealing with the Black man's plight and the psychological implications of marginalization.

The biblical text and Black psychology

By Christian theology the Black man is challenged to engage with how Jesus' teaching can be applied to himself and his community. This call is not to be read as a case for proselytizing. Certainly, as a pastor, I encourage it – but the theologian and pragmatist in me believes that the Bible is a profound text, a meditation on the meaning of the good life and how to live it. As such, an approach to Jesus' injunction to love oneself accepts the seriousness of this teaching as an antidote to the crises in which Black men are mired. Conversely, loving oneself transcends the elements relating to positive psychology and having a positive mental attitude, though such disciplines have their place. Rather, as is taught within African cosmology, of which the Black Church is a part, self-love requires coming to terms with a spirituality, a nonmaterial force, that permeates all affairs, human and nonhuman. This aspect of spirituality is expounded by Joseph Cervantes and Thomas Parham in 'Toward a Meaningful Spirituality for People of Color: Lessons for the Counselling Practitioner' (2005). They believe that spirituality is anchored in, and affects, life in all its fullness. One must remember that, although the West compartmentalizes existence, the same is not true in so-called 'developing countries', where the material and immaterial coexist as inseparable.

Self-love begins in the mind and must continue with an acknowledgement of how the Black man views himself – as an individual belonging to a collective and created in the image of God.

This must be a candid introspective process, but it must also involve a mode of extrospection. Loving oneself, and radically so, might prove a painful chasm to cross for some Black men and they might wish not to begin the journey towards self-love, though desiring it. On many occasions, those sharing Caribbean history or Black literature with other Black men have been faced with this response. Many, as they are invited to negotiate and discover themselves, are faced with a deep-seated anxiety that they will end up hating White people. White male hegemony has caused much suffering to Black lives, yet despite the possibility of gaining some autonomy, grabbing their life's rei(g)ns, they fear hating the one who has oppressed them. They are held back by fear and intense anxiety over their own self-understanding. This reaction gives some indication of how much Black men have been made impotent by White supremacist tyranny, with being unknowingly willing to defer to hegemonic White masculinity while harbouring anger, doubt and self-loathing among its lethal consequences.

Erica McInnis, a clinical psychologist, writes persuasively in 'Understanding African Beingness and Becoming' about how Black people can benefit from an African psychology. Her focus is to

> envision what black people's optimal self would look like if it
> had not been colonized and overlaid by a Eurocentric frame-

work of normality, and to pursue the trajectory that enslavement and colonization interrupted, with advances then far superior to those in the West in healing, and economic and spiritual wellbeing. (McInnis, 2018, p. 28)

McInnis makes it clear that Black psychology is not anti-White even though White psychology is anti-Black. She is informed by Wade Nobles (1986), an African American psychologist who asserts that what is essential for Black people is 'African Beingness' and African culture's reclamation, re-ascension, revitalization and affirmation. Nobles stresses this as a corrective challenge to Eurocentric psychology. McInnis uses African symbols/artefacts in her sessions to connect with her African diasporan clients. For the African-centred model of the African self, for example, McInnis develops the divine self as a spiritual self, having a purpose in life. Within the Christian context, Black people are seen as being created in the image of God, but adorned in black skin. As God created humankind in his image, so too must God be represented by Black people as Black, for 'God has created man in such a way that man's own destiny is inseparable from his relation to the creator' (Cone, 1997, p. 156).

Practical Black self-love

While McInnis makes pivotal strides in employing an African-centred model to help in conscientizing and healing Black people, there remains a problem for many African Caribbean people. Due to the transatlantic slave trade *Maafa* (a Kiswahili word meaning 'great tragedy'), many are far removed from an African heritage, with little or no direct cultural connection with anything African. Similarly, some African Caribbean people who were born and raised in the UK and are alienated by British culture find their connections to the Caribbean are figurative and tangential, despite the tenacious historical memory contained in reggae, calypso and various patois.

As a counsellor, psychologist, pastor, theologian and a Black man myself, I want to speak to Black men about six practical things they can do to develop self-love in line with the recommendations of Deborah Khoshaba (2012):

1 It would be prudent to **live your life for yourself and your relations**, rather than for the anxieties, insecurities, and stereotypes White men hold about you. As noted by both Baldwin (1955) and Fanon (1986), the White man's psychopathology is neither your responsibility nor your problem. Thus to consciously reject his negative commentaries and stereotypes is to give yourself a quality of power and live a conscious life affirming your humanity for yourself and your relations.

2 As a Black man, **act on what you know you need** and resist those things in a consumerist, demoralized and despiritualized White society that you know to be harmful to you.

3 **Practise good self-care**, which is achieved by exercise, having a good and balanced diet, getting enough sleep, and being with like-minded people. If you love yourself as your neighbour, treat yourself like you matter.

4 **Set boundaries** not for others but for yourself, by being cautious around people, situations and environments that deplete your good energy. After all, as Jesus admonished, 'do not ... cast your pearls before swine' (Matthew 7.6, New King James Version).

5 **Learn to forgive yourself.** Self-loathing traits such as perfectionism and self-contempt when things go wrong are absolutisms in all their forms. One way to work on self-loathing is to develop journalling skills or self-reflection that enable you to learn from what is happening in your life. Such lessons, well learnt, increase maturity, self-understanding and are of immense value for life and living.

6 **Live with focus and intention.** In other words, let self-discipline not give way to asceticism as you continually discover the love and joy in all things, large and small – the things bringing joy, happiness, and responsibility to and for your life.

Conclusion

Within a society wrestling with race, racialization and racism, the Black man's body remains a property, a thing, a sexualized object, a site upon which violence is visited, and a 'thing' presumed emotionally inept and intellectually deprived. After all these years, the Black man is still considered, by society at large, to be both 'less than' and 'other than'. In other words, non-human. The Black man's being has become a straw horse in the tribal conflict between White men and women, who are locked in a struggle over and between class, pay and gender. In addition, there is a prevailing Eurocentric blindness that is resistant to seeing the Black man as human. While the Black male is caught in this imposed vice, hundreds of years of conditioning have left a psychological and ugly emotional keloid, difficult to hide and even more difficult to remove.

There is no shortcut to accepting oneself, but one must recognize that, after all the Black man has experienced since his severance from his home, he is still here in the West. The Black man's existence testifies to the fact that while Black men are resilient, we have paid a steep price for living and for aspiring towards a future where we are autonomous and take wilful, intentional action towards our wellbeing. Since no one else will bear it for us, this is, this must be, our burden and responsibility alone.

Questions for further reflection

1 Why do you think that Black men seem to be objects of fear in the minds of many people throughout the Western world? Give some valid reasons for your thoughts.
2 Lack of self-love is a common theme for many people. Why do you believe this is so and how do you think it is possible that we can learn to love ourselves?
3 Why do you think the importance of self-love is seldom spoken about in our churches?

Bibliography

Akbar, N. (1992), *Visions for Black Men*, London: Mind Productions.

Allen, T. and Jackson, K. (producers), and Bourne, S. C. (director) (1996), *John Henrik Clarke: A great and mighty walk*, documentary, Lusaka: Black Dot Media.

Baldwin, J. (1955), 'Stranger in the Village', in J. Baldwin, *Notes of a Native Son*, Boston: Beacon Press, pp. 159–75.

Baldwin, J. (1961), *No One Knows My Name: More notes of a native son*, New York: Knopf Doubleday Publishing Group.

Baldwin, J. (1966). 'A Report from Occupied Territory', *The Nation*, https://www.thenation.com/article/report-occupied-territory/ (accessed 1.10.2021).

Baldwin, J. (1990), *Another Country*, New York: Penguin Books.

Ball, J., Milmo, D. and Ferguson, B. (2012), 'Half of UK's young black males are unemployed', *The Guardian,* 9 March 2012, https://www.theguardian.com/society/2012/mar/09/half-uk-young-black-men-un employed (accessed 1.11.2019).

Beckford, R. (2000), *Dread and Pentecostal: A political theology for the Black church in Britain*, Eugene, OR: Wipf and Stock Publishers.

Beckford, R. (2001), *God of the Rahtid: Redeeming rage*, London: Darton, Longman & Todd.

Blades, L. A. (2016), 'Trauma from slavery can actually be passed down through your genes', *Teen Vogue*, https://www.teenvogue.com/story/slavery-trauma-inherited-genetics (accessed 1.10.2021).

Buck-Morss, S. (2009), *Hegel, Haiti, and Universal History*, Pittsburgh, PA: University of Pittsburgh Press.

Burrell, T. (2010), *Brainwashed: Challenging the myth of Black inferiority*, London: Smiley Books.

Campbell, D. (2018), 'Black medics in NHS paid less than white medics', *The Guardian*, 27 September 2018, https://www.theguardian.com/society/2018/sep/27/black-medics-in-nhs-paid-thousands-less-than-white-medics (accessed 2.7.2019).

Cassuto, L. (1996), *The Inhuman Race: The racial grotesque in African American literature and culture*, New York: Columbia University Press.

Cervantes, J. and Parham, T. A. (2005), 'Toward a Meaningful Spirituality for People of Color: Lessons for the Counselling Practitioner', *Cultural Diversity and Ethnic Minority Psychology*, 11(1), pp. 69–81, https://doi.org/10.1037/1099-9809.11.1.69 (accessed 1.7.2019).

Clarke, J. H. (1974), *Black Americans, Immigrants Against Their Will*, Atlanta, GA: Atlanta University Press.

Coates, T. (2015), *Between the World and Me*, Melbourne: The Text Publishing Company.

Coleman, A. (2017), 'Stealing eternity: The Black conscious movement's dangerous misrepresentation of Christianity', The K.I.N.G. Movement, 25 September 2017, http://www.kingmovement.com/stealing-eternity-black-conscious-movements-dangerous-misrep resentation-christianity/ (accessed 30.9.2021).

Cole-Rous, J. (n.d.), The eunuch of Ethiopia. *Journey Online*, http://globalchristiancenter.com/christian-living/lesser-known-bible-peo ple/31308-the-eunuch-of-ethiopia (accessed 1.11.2019).

Cone, J. (1997), *Black Theology and Black Power*, New York: Orbis Books.

Cone, J. (2017), *The Black Theology of Liberation*, New York: Orbis Books.

Cone, J. (2020), *The Black Theology of Liberation. 50th Anniversary Edition*, New York: Orbis Books.

Cox, O. (2001), 'Class, caste and race: A study in social dynamics', in E. Cashmore and J. Jennings (eds), *Racism: Essential readings*, London: Sage Publications, pp. 49–74.

Croxford, R. (2018), 'Ethnic minority academics earn less than white colleagues', BBC, 7 December, https://www.bbc.co.uk/news/education-46473269 (accessed 19.8.2019).

Curry, T. J. (2017), *The Man-Not: Race, Class, Genre, and the Dilemmas of Black Manhood*, Philadelphia, PA: Temple University Press.

DeGruy, J. (2005), *Post Traumatic Slave Syndrome: America's Legacy of Enduring Injury and Healing*, Portland, OR: Joy DeGruy Publications Inc.

Des Pres, T. (1980a), *An Anatomy of Life in the Death Camps*, Oxford: Oxford University Press.

Des Pres, T. (1980b), *The Survivor: Life in the death camps*, Oxford University Press.

Exum, J. C. (2002), '*Lethal woman 2*: Reflections on Delilah and her incarnation as Liz Hurley,', in M. O'Kane (ed.), *Borders, Boundaries and the Bible*, Sheffield: Sheffield University Press, pp. 254–73.

Fanin, I. (2017), 'Is there institutional racism in mental health care?' BBC, 5 July 2017, https://www.bbc.co.uk/news/health-40495539 (accessed 3.9.2019).

Fanon, F. (1967), *The Wretched of the Earth*, London: Penguin Books.

Fanon, F. (1986), *Black Skin, White Masks*, London: Pluto Press (original work published 1952).

Figueira, D. M. (1994), *The Exotic: A decadent quest*, New York: New York Press.

Foley, N. (2020), *Unemployment by Ethnic Background* (Briefing Paper No. 6385), retrieved from the UK Parliament's House of Commons Library website: https://commonslibrary.parliament.uk/research-briefings/sn06385/ (accessed 1.12.2020).

Fredrickson, G. (1987), *The Black Image in the White Mind: The debate on Afro-American character and destiny, 1817–1914*, Middletown, CT: Wesleyan University Press.

Fryer, P. (1984), *Staying Power: The History of Black People in Britain*, London: Pluto Press.

Garvey, M. (1986), *The Philosophy and Opinions of Marcus Garvey, or, Africa for the Africans* (Vol. 1), Houston, TX: The Majority Press.

Giga, S., Hoel, H. and Lewis, D. (2008), *A review of Black and minority ethnic (BME) employee experiences of workplace bullying*, Bradford: University of Bradford, https://www.researchgate.net/publication/260246604_A_Review_of_Black_and_Minority_Eth nic_BME_Employee_Experiences_of_Workplace_Bullying (accessed 1.6.2020).

Gilroy, P. (2013), *There Ain't No Black in the Union Jack: The politics of race and the nation*, London: Routledge (original work published 2002).

Goodman, A. (2017), 'Newly discovered 1964 MLK speech on civil rights, segregation and Apartheid South Africa', *Democracy Now*, 16 January 2017, https://soundcloud.com/democracynow/part-3-newly-discovered-1964-mlk-speech-on-civil-rights-segregation-apartheid-south-africa (accessed 2.4.2020).

Griggs, C. (1990), *Early Egyptian Christianity: From its origins to 451 C.E.*, Leiden: Brill.

Hall, M. (2011), 'Negotiating Jamaican masculinities', in R. Jackson III and M. Balaji (eds), *Global Masculinities and Manhood*, Champaign, IL: University of Illinois Press, pp. 31–51.

Hall, S. and Schwarz, B. (2017), 'Familiar Stranger: A Life Between Two Islands', in Stuart Hall, *Selected Writings on Race and Difference*, London: Penguin Books.

Hill, R. (ed.) (1990), *The Marcus Garvey and Universal Negro Improvement Association Papers, Vol. VII: November 1927–August 1940*, Oaktown, CA: University of California Press.

Huggan, G. (2001), *The Postcolonial Exotic: Marketing the margins*, London: Routledge.

The Human Rights and Equality Commission's Report (2018), *Is Britain Fairer?*, London: Human Rights and Equality Commission.

Jackson, R., III (2006) *Scripting the Black Masculine Body: Identity, discourse, and racial politics in popular media*, Albany, NY: State University of New York Press.

Jordan, W. (1977), *White Over Black: American attitudes toward the Negro, 1550–1812*, London: W. W. Norton.

Kauffman, M. (2017), *Black Tudors: The untold story*, London: Oneworld Publications.

Khoshaba, D. (2012), 'A seven-step prescription for self-love', *Psychology Today*, 27 March 2012, https://www.psychologytoday.com/gb/

blog/get-hardy/201203/seven-step-prescription-self-love (accessed 1.8.2018).

Krystal, J. (2016), 'Trauma's epigenetic fingerprint observed in children of Holocaust survivors', *Elsevier*, 1 September 2016, https://www. elsevier.com/about/press-releases/archive/research-and-journals/traumas-epigenetic-fingerprint-observed-in-children-of-holocaust-survivors (accessed 30.9.2021).

Kuo, R. (2015), '6 reasons why "bad Asians" rock and "positive" racial stereotypes need to go', *Everyday Feminism*, 28 November 2015, http://everydayfeminism.com/2015/11/positive-stereotypes-still-bad/ (accessed 10.4.2020).

Kuo, R. (2016), '4 reasons why calling a woman of color "exotic" is racist', *Everyday Feminism*, 26 January 2016, http://everydayfemi nism.com/2016/01/calling-woc-exotic-is-racist/ (accessed 1.5.2020).

Linebaugh, P. and Rediker, M. (2013), *The Many-headed Hydra: Sailors, slaves, commoners, and the hidden history of the revolutionary Atlantic*, Boston, MA: Beacon Press.

Longhi, S., and Brynin, M. (2017), *The Ethnicity Pay Gap*, Institute of Social and Economic Research, Essex, UK: University of Essex, https://www.equalityhumanrights.com/sites/default/files/research-report-108-the-ethnicity-pay-gap.pdf (accessed 1.5.2020).

Lyons, C. H. (1975), *To Wash an Aethiopian White: British ideas about Black African educability, 1530–1960*, New York: Teachers College Press.

MacDougall, H. A. (1982), *Racial Myth in English History: Trojans, Teutons, and Anglo-Saxons*, Irvine, CA: Harvest House Publishers.

Malcolm X. (1970), *By Any Means Necessary*, College Park, GA: Pathfinder Press.

Marley, B. (1980), 'Redemption Song', *Uprising*, Jamaica: Tuff Gong Island.

Mbiti, J. (1990), *African Religions and Philosophy*, Portsmouth, NH: Heinemann Publishers.

Mbiti, J. (2015), *Introduction to African Religion*, 2nd edn, Long Grove, IL: Waveland Press.

McInnis, E. M. (2018), 'Understanding African Beingness and Becoming', *Therapy Today*, 29(8), pp. 28–31, https://library.laredo.edu/eds/detail?db=a9h&an=132445483&isbn=17487846 (accessed 2.12.2020).

Moynihan, D. P. (1965), *The Negro Family: The Case for National Action*, Washington, DC: US Government Printing Office.

Nobles, W. (1986), *African Psychology: Toward its reclamation, reascension and revitalization*, Oakland, CA: Institute for the Advanced Study of Black Family Life and Culture.

Onyeka (2013), *Blackamoores: Africans in Tudor England: Their presence, status, and origins*, London: Narrative Eye.

Oxford English Dictionary (n.d.), *Oxford English Dictionary*, Oxford: Oxford University Press, retrieved 26.11.2020 from www.oed.com.

Pinn, A. (2003), *Terror and Triumph: The nature of Black religion*, Minneapolis, MN: Fortress Press.

Poliakov, L. (1974), *Aryan Myth: A history of racist and nationalist ideas in Europe*, Falmer, East Sussex: Sussex University Press.

Reid-Salmon, D. (2012), *Burning for Freedom: A theology for the Black Atlantic struggle for liberation*, Kingston: Ian Randle Publishers.

Roberts, D. (2011), *Fatal Invention: How science, politics, and big business re-create race in the twenty-first century*, New York: New Press.

Roper, G. (2015), 'Sam Sharpe in the context of the struggle for freedom and equality in the Caribbean: Freedom, innate desire or acquired appetite', *American Baptist Quarterly*, 34(1), pp. 86–97, https://ixtheo.de/Record/1647196590 (accessed 12.4.2017).

Russell Group (2018), *Our Universities*, https://russellgroup.ac.uk/about/our-universities/ (accessed 30.9.2021).

Said, E. (1979), *Orientalism*, New York: Vintage Books.

Smith, H. (2017). 'Nine in every 10,000 Black Britons spend time in youth custody, says Ministry of Justice report', *The Independent*, 1 September 2017, https://www.independent.co.uk/news/uk/crime/young-offenders-black-british-people-more-likely-prison-time-nine-10000-ministry-justice-report-a7924156.html (accessed 20.4.2021).

Spencer, W. D. (1998), *Dread Jesus*, London: SPCK.

St. George's University Hospital (2018), *Ethnicity Pay Gap 2018/19*, https://www.stgeorges.nhs.uk/wp-content/uploads/2020/03/Ethnicity-Pay-Gap-2018-19.pdf (accessed 1.4.2021).

Sweet, J. H. (2003), *Recreating Africa: Culture, Kinship, and Religion in the African-Portuguese World, 1441–1770*, Chapel Hill, NC: University of North Carolina Press.

The Assembly of the British Council of Churches (1976), *The New Black Presence in Britain: A Christian scrutiny*, London: Community and Race Relations Unit of the British Council of Churches.

Therrin, A. (2018), 'Ethnic minority consultants "paid less" than white colleagues', BBC, https://www.bbc.co.uk/news/health-45421437 (accessed 12.4.2021).

Thurman, H. (1996), *Jesus and the Disinherited*, Boston, MA: Beacon Press.

Topping, A., Barr, C. and Duncan, P. (2018), 'Gender pay gap figures reveal eight in 10 UK firms pay men more', *The Guardian*, 4 April 2018, https://www.theguardian.com/money/2018/apr/04/gender-pay-gap-figures-reveal-eight-in-10-uk-firms-pay-men-more (accessed 10.7.2021).

Ubani, L. (2011), *Afrikan Mind Reconnection and Spiritual Re-awakening*, Vol. 1, Bloomington, IN: Xlibris Corporation.

Wood, M. (2012), 'Britain's first black community in Elizabethan

London', BBC, https://www.bbc.co.uk/news/magazine-18903391 (accessed 20.9.2021).

Woodson, C. G. (2009). *The Mis-education of the Negro*, Scotts Valley, CA: CreateSpace Independent Publishing.

Yancy, G. (2018), 'The Ugly Truth about Being a Black Professor in America', *The Chronicle*, https://www.chronicle.com/article/the-ugly-truth-of-being-a-black-professor-in-america (accessed 20.9.2021).

Yehuda, R. (2015), 'How trauma and resilience cross generations', https://onbeing.org/programs/rachel-yehuda-how-trauma-and-resil ience-cross-generations-nov2017/ (accessed 20.9.2021).

7

Black Theology and the Care of the Soul, Mind and Body: Reading African American Theology from a Black British Perspective

Introduction

There are Black people from the African diaspora concerned about the life and plight of Black people in the West. In this chapter are reflections on the origins of Black theology, a brief psychological examination of the transatlantic slave trade and the cost experienced by being severed from one's place of birth and its impact on one's being and identity. In addition, some considerations will be given to violence being used as a form of social control and its devastating effect on Black humanity. What is often forgotten is that African Caribbean people in the UK have historical roots in the slave trade. Thus there are strong connections with the African American experience.

In more recent times, Black Christian voices have emerged within the UK context from the Windrush epoch, vying for a Black theological anthropology, but making a plea to be included in the transatlantic dialogue with their American and Caribbean siblings. In the final analysis, there is an impassioned appeal for Black theology not to clamber for admittance and acceptance into the White academy, because Black theology, by its nature, is a theology for marginalized peoples as well as offering freedom for the worried well, the powerful and the rich.

The origins of Black theology

Arguably, the genesis of contemporary Black theology may be traced to Howard Thurman's classic text, *Jesus and the Disinherited*. Here, Thurman contends that folk 'whose backs were against the wall' were drawn to Jesus' liberative teachings (Thurman, 1976, p. 7). The consolidated work of Black theology continues with James Cone, who, in observing Black life in White America, asked the question (Cone, 1997, p. xvi), what does God have to say about the suffering of Black people? Using a Marxist paradigm and interrogating the Black Power movement, Cone devised a set of principles giving rise to Black theology. Although originally understood as a political theology, I contend that, by implication, Black theology is also a pastoral theology. By pastoral theology, I mean a theology that concerns itself with the care and cure of souls. In a nutshell, pastoral theology is the integration of psychology and theology which is more nuanced than simply applying psychology in a random manner to the world of theology.

In *Liberating our Dignity, Saving Our Souls*, Lee Butler reasons that mainstream psychology panders to White supremacy notions and Black inferiority. Psychology that is relevant for Black people is emphasized by Butler: 'Black (African) psychology is a field dedicated to the analysis of the systems of oppression that inhibit black life for the sole purpose of liberating African people' (Butler, 2006, p. 127). From another perspective, Stewart Hiltner, considered the founding father of pastoral theology, defined it as 'a shepherding dimension to the total aspect of church life and ministry followed by some theological reflections' (Hiltner, 1958, p. 20). In contrast to Hiltner's mainstream understanding, Carroll Watkins Ali, an African American female pastoral theologian, argues for a pastoral theology taking into consideration the cultural and historical context of African Americans. Watkins Ali writes of 'theological reflection on the cultural context as relevant for strategic pastoral care giving in the context of ministry' (Watkins Ali, 1999, p. 10). A further perspective of this brand of pastoral theology is 'its heart is an interpretive dialectic between theological anthropology and psychology that results in a definitive understanding of humanity' (Butler, 2006, pp. 127–9).

Cone's observation highlighted that the so-called 'problem' was Black people's innate desire to be treated as equal to their White counterparts. In reality, the experience of Black people in the USA is illustrated in the words of psychologist William James, who likened the experience of being ignored to that of being 'cut dead':

> No more fiendish punishment could be devised, were such a thing physically possible, than that one should be turned loose in society and remain absolutely unnoticed by all the members thereof. If no one turned around when we entered, answered when we spoke, or minded what we did, but if every person we met 'cut us dead,' and acted as if we were non-existing things, a kind of rage and impotent despair would before long well up in us, from which the cruellest bodily torture would be a relief. (James, 1890, p. 239)

This stark definition highlights Black humanity's plight in America as being a disposable nonentity, similar to Du Bois' colour line concept being a problem in America. The African American's plight links them to their oft-forgotten siblings in the Caribbean and the UK, and even more so now in different parts of Europe.

Detachment from home: Black humanity in the West

The African diaspora has its roots in the violence encountered in the transatlantic slave trade. However, an alternative argument exists in which Ivan Van Sertima makes the claim, supported by archaeological and historical evidence, that there was an African presence in America and other parts of the world from around 1310 (Van Sertima, 1976, p. 142).

Reflecting on the African diaspora inhabiting the landmasses of the West draws attention to the uniqueness of the former enslaved African. One aspect uniting the disparate enslaved and dispersed African groups is the Middle Passage: the horrendous journey by which enslaved Africans, in their millions, were transported to lands where they lived in terror. This violent removal from one's land cannot be taken lightly. What is often overlooked is the psychological, emotional, spiritual and existential effect on the enslaved as they were forcibly removed from their homeland. This wrenching from the land has not been given much thought. Psychologists, psychotherapists and the like are acutely aware of the potential devastation of the beginnings of a child's life if they are rejected or do not bond well with their mothers or are continually rejected by their significant other. It has many effects, including a low sense of self, low mood and a distorted worldview, coupled with poor relationship development (Bowlby, 1969, p. 194). If compensatory measures are not quickly established, the relationship between mother and child is set to be difficult, with complications later in life. This important bonding is conceptualized in attachment theory, where 'attachment is a deep and enduring emotional bond that connects one person to another across time and space' (Salcuni, 2015, p. 4).

Attachment theory's chief proponent was psychiatrist John Bowlby, who, while studying the relationship between mother and child, observed distress in children when separated from their mother. He later defined attachment as a 'lasting psychological connectedness between human beings' (Bowlby, 1969, p. 194).

Using the same idea, one wonders whether a violent severance from one's homeland evokes significant negative effect on the captured and dispersed, with potential debilitating outcomes, partially or totally unknown, and with lingering consequences affecting the formerly enslaved progenitors. Howard Thurman offers some insight into the devastation of such removal from one's homeland:

Unlike the American Indian, the African slave was uprooted from his land, his territory, and brought forcibly several thousand miles away to another land completely alien to his spirit and his gods. All ties that gave him a sense of belonging, of counting, of being a person nourished by a community of persons were abruptly severed, lacerated, torn asunder. Bodies that were emotionally bleeding hulks were set down in the new world of the Americas. Initially he had no standing, even that of an outsider. In terms of his access to the sources of nourishment for community, initially he had none. No. Not even the status of a human being. It is no accident that the New Testament Greek word for slave is *soma*, which means body, thing. (Thurman, 1998, p. 281)

Thurman's 129-word description is chillingly cold as the enslaved African is reduced to a 'thing'. His comment is made without any reference to psychological analysis that would add further insight into the human cost of violent severance from one's homeland. Furthermore, detachment from Africa was not just detachment from lands that the enslaved had recently inhabited. They had occupied their lands for many centuries. The severance from their homeland was one thing, but the gratuitous violence they encountered was unprecedented.

The use of violence as a form of social control and its impact on Black humanity

Jamaican sociologist Orlando Patterson refers to the violence used on the plantations as a form of social control and the whole treatment experienced as natal alienation (Patterson, 1982, p. 7). These are not fancy words used to describe an abstract human phenomenon; ultimately they describe the situation of millions of human beings whose lives, culture, history and language had been ravaged.

It was evident how violence was used as a regular measure on the plantations to keep the enslaved in check. Teresa L. Amott and Julie A. Matthaei demonstrate, in *Race, Gender, and Work: A Multi-cultural Economic History of Women in the United States*, how violence was used as a painful deterrent. They emphasize that 'Slavery was built on coercion and violence. Slave owners continually resorted to physical intimidation and punishment to keep slaves from rebelling and slaves continually resisted enslavement' (Amott and Matthaei, 1996, p. 145). Trevor Burnard's thinking on the slave masters' complicated sexual antics during the eighteenth century also deserves serious consideration. He writes:

> The psychological damage suffered by the slaves living under traumatizing conditions and in a radically unstable society was especially apparent in slaves' sexual interactions. The tyranny that slaveholders exercised over their slaves, the constant dehumanizing that slaves experienced under that tyranny, and the extreme instability and violence that marked plantation slavery brutalized slaves. Subjected to constant violence themselves, they were quick to resort to violence against each other. The result was that slaves found it difficult to maintain order in their own communities, especially since they emulated their masters in giving little respect to the integrity of established slave relationships. (Burnard, 1998, pp. 181–2)

The brutal living reality of enslavement could not have been imagined by the enslaved. This unexpected treatment led to a severe relationship breakdown which made the forming of a stable community impossible, and thus reinforced the notion of 'Who am I, and where do I belong?'

While this chapter has focused on the impact of enslavement in America and the Caribbean, it must not be forgotten, although it often is, that the African diaspora found in the UK shares the communal history – the horrific sojourn of the Middle Passage, severance from African homeland, dehumanization and the employment of violence on the black body and psyche. Thus the ties binding a person to their original culture, history, language and so forth were further weakened as many arrived, by invitation of the then Conservative government, to rebuild Britain after World War II. The Windrush epoch saw 492 Caribbeans, mainly Jamaicans, arrive in the UK, with vigour and zeal to help rebuild the motherland and earnest to embrace and be fully accepted into British life and culture (John, 1976, p. 7). What began with great expectation and a desire to integrate was met, by and large, with great hostility.

A UK Black theological anthropological identity

Conversations about Black identity have been ongoing for some time, with a conference being held in 1945 by the Pan-African movement. This conference had many great names in attendance but was, it seems, not worthy of much historical acknowledgement as they conducted their conference in the shadow of the decline of the British Empire. However, on arrival and unbeknown to them and the British population, the Windrush generation was about to cause an unexpected social and religious stir in the UK. This upheaval is reflected upon by Walter Hollenweger as he writes in Roswith Gerloff's classic text *A Plea for Black British Theologies*: 'Christians in Britain prayed for many years for revival, and when it came, they did not recognize it because it was black. Nevertheless, it produced a religious, social and intellectual vitality which is astonishing' (Gerloff, 1992, p. ix).

Empire Windrush

The now infamous invitation, 'Come to Sunny Britain', is humorously quoted by the Caribbean migrants as they retell their stories of enticement to come to the UK. Received myths were shattered when they arrived in Britain and realized the streets were not paved with gold as they had been indoctrinated in the Caribbean. Here were migrants, invited into the UK to help rebuild a land where their ancestors were instrumental in developing the nation via a catastrophic loss of life on the many plantations in the Americas. This land, the UK, had been decimated by White men who were at odds with each other, and cheap labour was needed to rebuild the motherland. Many Caribbeans came, not realizing that they had been somewhat deluded and duped. A new identity was being created in the Caribbean and for many it was disrupted when they took up the offer of migrating to the UK. Arriving as integrationists, they soon saw that things were not as they had been told (Hill, 1958, p. 19). Mother England, as they had been taught, was an illusion. Their new identity being formed in the Caribbean was being disrupted and became more complex as the new arrivals to the UK were now twice removed from Africa and again relocated to another part of an alien West. This detachment and its consequence have slipped under the radar of African Caribbean consciousness and existence in the UK. Furthermore, this detachment was further exacerbated as they arrived in Britain, a land which was not theirs. For Caribbeans, arrival in the UK by invitation guaranteed full British rights, because they were still under British colonial rule and therefore were British subjects. In reality, this was not so. The recent public outcry in the UK in April 2018 by politicians and many of the Windrush epoch and their descendants, some of whom were deported back to Jamaica, proves just how vulnerable the colonial children were on arrival in the UK (BBC, 2018, 'Windrush Scandal').

The African Caribbean people were, in reality, 'landless people'. Historian of Black religion Charles Long conceptualized this notion of landless people as belonging to African American people 'where the image of Africa as it appears in black religion is unique, for the black people in America are a landless people' (Long, 1997, p. 26). Coupled with Long's treatise is the argument made by the late African American historian, John Henrik Clarke, 'that black people must understand that Western civilization was not created with them in mind' (Clarke, 1996). This notion has not yet been fully explored. One of the few voices reflecting on this matter comes from Ghanaian pastoral theologian Emmanuel Lartey, who says: 'The effects of Black existence in Britain upon Black people have yet to be fully worked out' (Lartey, 1999, p. 79).

To examine Black life in the UK, psychotherapy can be used as a constructive discipline to explore the overrepresentation of mental illness in the UK's psychiatric system. The data can be used to develop an understanding of the mental health and well-being experienced by the African Caribbean community living in the UK. One wonders whether being twice removed from their African cultural homeland and subsequent generations being born in a land not designed for them creates an often unspoken, but ongoing, experience of unease and tension. For example, many Caribbeans in the UK have little regard for Africa, and many born in the UK are removed from the Caribbean, yet do not feel at home in England. Worse still, if they go to the Caribbean, they are regarded as foreigners and, in the UK context, their colour makes them stand out and not blend in with the host population. Despite the welcome some received, and the societal coldness felt by many, there were some Black people who felt the harshness of landing in Britain and began to write about the pain of their experience in the UK.

Emerging Black voices within the UK

With a significant lapse of time outside and inside the church setting, we begin to hear Black Christian voices reflecting theologically on their experience of being Black and living in the UK. One of the earliest voices was that of Sam Selvon's *Lonely Londoners* (1956). Selvon does not reflect theologically on life for Black people in Britain, but his work contains religious themes. For example, he refers to people meeting on Sundays to gain strength and encouragement from each other (Selvon, 1956, p. 135). Later, Venetia Newall records the Caribbean migratory experience as one of 'withdrawal and cultural retention' (Newall, 1975, pp. 28–9).

In 1976, the Church of England commissioned a study to examine why they had lost so many Anglican adherents when they arrived in the UK, despite having endorsement letters testifying that they were bona fide members of the Church of England. The church failed to see Caribbean Christians as their brothers and sisters, and in doing so failed to capture their gifts and the contributions they would have made which would have enriched the church. The study showed how 'Black people's presence evoked a sense of "dis-ease" within British society, but it highlighted fissures existing prior to Caribbean migration.' These were some of the further findings:

> Black people cannot allow White society to dictate the terms of analysis of their situation in Britain, nor give the prescriptions. As Black people continue to adhere to White society for antidotes for their deliverance it continues to enhance their destruction, yet for effective change to occur the marginalized and the poor must make changes for themselves. (John, 1976, p. 7)

The study did not advocate a segregationist approach for Black Christians in the UK, but it recorded that 'being a part of a system where one is alienated is madness, and attempting to join such a system and to bring about change from within when your humanity is ignored and not accepted, is double madness' (John, 1976, p. 17).

In 1986, Anita Jackson interviewed five pastors from various denominations. The overriding theme from the publication was the great need for autonomy. One pastor said, 'West Indians in England need to get off their backside and do something and stop expecting things to come into their lap' (Jackson, 1985, p. 58). Following Jackson's publication, Ira Brooks, a New Testament Church of God pastor, reflecting on Black life in Britain, became frustrated with his organization as he studied and discovered the depth and richness of African civilizations before the arrival of European missionaries. He challenged his own organization for their silence in the face of racism and its problem in the church while arguing for a 'contextual theology that represented their views about God' (Brooks, 1986, pp. 38–51).

The early 1990s saw a proliferation of publications wrestling with the issue of racism, inclusion and the Christian faith. Paul Grant and Raj Patel argued for Black people to 'take responsibility for their faith journey, their development and the creation of a theology for Black people by Black people' (Grant and Patel, 1990, p. 1). However, the most concise publication arguing for and developing a Black British theology was cultural critic and Black theologian Robert Beckford's *Jesus is Dread*. Building on numerous authors, Beckford stressed the inherent inadequacy of Western theological models to capture the experiences of Black Christians. Furthermore, he referred to the Black Church, Black worship and its healing nature in this way: 'Worshipping in a Black Majority Church kept me sane as a Black person of African Caribbean descent in Britain' (Beckford, 1998, pp. 4–5).

While Beckford opened the development of a Black British theology in his seminal work, the most prolific writer on Black British theology is, without doubt, Anthony Reddie. Reddie has used a variety of exercises, drama and a rereading of the biblical text to teach and introduce ideas of Black theology to Black British adherents. For example, in *Nobodies to Somebodies* (2003), Reddie introduces ideas from Black and Liberation theology to train a wide range of ministerial practitioners. In developing a Black British theology, Reddie has valiantly attempted to articulate a Black British theology that encapsulates the Atlantic, but in so doing he has omitted an important voice in the dialogue. This omission is taken up by Delroy Reid-Salmon, who praises Reddie's contribution, but offers the critique that currently, a Black British theology is an African American voice in a Black British body and a 'closer relationship with their Caribbean siblings would be more beneficial' (Reid-Salmon, 2008, p. 135).

Thus three major African diasporic locations, all united by the horrors of enslavement and the Middle Passage, are attempting to work out an understanding of themselves in their context, but are seldom uniting in conversation.

The future for African American theology and Black theology

Is there a future for Black theology for the Black community? Alistair Kee (2017) seems to think not. He contends that when Black theology first appeared it was radical and revolutionary

but it has now lost its way, with the gap between wealthy educated Blacks and poor Blacks continuing to increase. While
Kee's analysis may have a measure of truth, it is fatal to allow
one person's comments to determine one's destiny.

Oppression and liberation remain key factors for Black
people requiring freedom. In moving forward, there are a few
matters to consider.

1 There must be a continual dialogue with other disciplines,
   while firmly committed to the biblical insights on the human
   condition. Black people, despite their many stereotypes and
   discriminatory experiences, are still human beings created in
   the image of God.
2 Black theology must take a firm grip on the shaping of identity.
3 The development of Black theology must find ways to
   develop an encouraging and nurturing dialogue with adherents of continental Africa and their offspring elsewhere.
4 Black theology is not arguing for separatism but it cannot
   afford to join with the White academy. Adherence to powerful institutions inevitably ensures that such a potentially
   revolutionary theology loses its potency due to the policies
   and procedures laid down to govern what is taught and how
   it is taught. Black theology cannot expend precious energy
   vying for acceptance and legitimization in White institutions
   that, due to fear, lack of understanding and White dominance, will inevitably and eventually disempower it.
5 Another reason for resisting acceptance within the academy
   is this: 'There is simply too much blood in the water.' Too
   many lives of the enslaved African ancestors have been lost,
   not only in labouring to provide sugar, tobacco and cotton,
   but millions of lives were cut short and 'cut dead'. Not only
   was there the loss of physical life, there was also the immense
   loss of human potential. The continual loss of Black human
   potential remains today, with an increasing overrepresentation of Black lives within the mental health system and the
   penal system, lack of employment and the ongoing lack of
   historical education about who Black people are.

6 Furthermore, given Black people's experience in the USA, exemplified by the killing of George Floyd by the state police, and Black life in the UK diaspora, Black theology must not be a theology only concerned with gaining recognition within the academy. There are too many existential issues continuing to plague, threaten and wreak havoc on Black life. In the USA, it would appear that Black life has been under constant threat, control, assault and surveillance since the first black sole of enslaved feet touched the soil of the Americas. Within the UK, the national move to sever itself from Europe via Brexit, in which it was successful, and the recent Windrush scandal are a stark reminder that Black people are still not readily welcomed here. In contrast, some have heralded the recent Royal Wedding in the UK, and the prominence of Black people who were so heavily featured during the ceremony as opening up a new day of racial inclusion for Britain. The wedding was only a day. Most Black people in the UK awoke the following morning wrestling with the same issues of race, hidden by the tentacles extended by class and power. Black theology must start from the grassroots, primarily to conscientize Black people to take full responsibility for their destiny.

7 Finally, the biggest stronghold confronting Black theology, with which it must fiercely grapple if it is going to have a robust future, is that of power. If Black theology is going to remain true to the biblical text in addressing the notions of power, there is a paradigm within the Scriptures that can be modelled. In the Sermon on the Mount (Matthew 5—7), Jesus gathered simple folk together as he expounded the principles of his Father's kingdom and how to live on the earth. One must remember that such teachings were expounded under a cruel, violent and oppressive Roman government (Goldsworthy, 2017). The point here is that a possible way of dealing with power and oppression is to educate and mobilize ordinary people. The end result of Jesus imparting life into these ordinary people was that 'they turned the world upside down' (Acts 17.6). Black theology was not conceptualized to turn the world upside

down, per se, but much can be accomplished if people are effectively equipped to live to their potential.

There is still much more work for Black theology to do. It is hard, blistering and thankless work, and dreadfully painful. However, if it is to be a theology bringing life to people, both oppressed and oppressor alike, it must rethink and act how it will appeal to the masses of Black people who call themselves Christians or people of faith.

Conclusion

Since the days of James Cone and his conceptualization of a Black theology of liberation, the world has shifted significantly. For example, in terms of technology we have evolved from the humble typewriter to the flexibility of electronic devices that enable dissertations and the like to be written quickly. The world in its various guises of class, race, ethnicities, sexual orientation and power has changed too. If Black theology, for the liberation of its people, is to remain a viable form of God-speak, it must wrestle with the issues of the day. Chiefly, it must contend and give answers to race, ethnicity, class, gender, sexuality and sexualities but most of all power, which affects all people.

An African American theology cannot remain an insular form of theology limited to the shores of its land; it must now lift up its head as 'the fields are ripe for harvesting' (John 4.35). There are millions of displaced Africans throughout the world who need conscientizing in lifting up their heads to tackle the issues of life on their shores. Rather than extending their reach for acceptance within the academy, a better use of energy will be to enter a meaningful transatlantic dialogue as equals with their UK and Caribbean siblings. Including African voices in the dialogue is also pivotal, as issues of dominance are significantly changing for them too. United we are strong, but divided we place ourselves on the path of failure in such changing and unpredictable times.

Questions for further reflection

1 What are your thoughts about the idea of 'colourizing' theology (having Black theology, White theology, etc.)?
2 The Old Testament was built upon diasporan people, and the New Testament was founded on a Church under persecution. Given the background of the Bible, how significant is this sacred book for oppressed people groups and why?
3 This chapter contends that it is not wise for Black theology to make a bid for inclusion in the halls of White academia because it will lose its potency. Discuss the case for all people groups being allowed to express their songs, worship and understanding of God in their own voices and not be dominated by another people group.

Bibliography

Ainsworth, M. D. S. (1973), 'The development of infant-mother attachment', in B. Cardwell and H. Ricciuti (eds), *Review of Child Development Research*, Chicago, IL: University of Chicago Press.

Amott, T. L. and Matthaei, J. A. (1996), *Race, Gender, and Work: A Multi-cultural Economic History of Women in the United States*, Boston: South End Press.

BBC (2018), 'Windrush Scandal', BBC News, 25 May 2018, http://www.bbc.co.uk/news/topics/c9vwmzw7n7lt/windrush-scandal (accessed 28.5.2018).

Beckford, R. (1998), *Jesus is Dread: Black Theology and Black Culture in Britain*, London: Darton, Longman & Todd.

Bowlby, J. (1969), *Attachment and Loss, Vol. 1, Attachment*, New York: Basic Books.

Brooks, V. I. (1986), *Another Gentleman to the Ministry*, Birmingham: Compeer Press.

Burnard, T. (1998), 'The sexual life of an eighteenth-century Jamaican slave overseer', in M. D. Smith (ed.), *Sex and Sexuality in Early America*, New York: New York University Press.

Butler, L. (2006), *Liberating Our Dignity, Saving Our Souls*, St Louis, MO: Chalice Press.

Clarke, Henrik, J. (1996), *A Long and Mighty Walk*, video directed by St. Clair Bourne, with John Henrik Clarke, Cheikh Anta Diop, Marcus Garvey, John F. Kennedy, https://www.youtube.com/watch?v=njdQzyQnHeg (accessed 30.9.2021).

Cone, J. (1997), *God of the Oppressed*, New York: Orbis Books.

Du Bois, E. B. W. (2015), *The Soul of Black Folks*, New Haven, CT: Yale University Press.

Gerloff, R. (1992), *A Plea for Black British Theologies: Volume 1: The Black Church Movement in Britain in Its Transatlantic Cultural and Theological Interaction with Special Reference to the Pentecostal Oneness (Apostolic) and Sabbatarian Movements*, Eugene, OR: Wipf and Stock Publishers.

Goldsworthy, A. (2017), *Pax Romana: War, Peace and Conquest in the Roman World*, London: Weidenfeld and Nicholson.

Grant, P. and Patel, R. (1990), *A Time to Speak: Perspectives of Black Christians in Britain*, Birmingham: Racial Justice and Black Theology Working Group.

Hill, C. (1958), *Black and White in Harmony: The Drama of West Indians in the Big City, from a London Minister's Notebook*, London: Hodder & Stoughton.

Hill, C. (1965), *How Colour Prejudiced is Britain?*, London: Victor Gollancz.

Hiltner, S. (1958), *Preface to Pastoral Theology*, New York: Abingdon Press.

Jackson, A. (1985), *Catching Both Sides of the Wind: Conversations with Five Black Pastors*, London: British Council of Churches.

James, W. (1890), *The Principles of Psychology, Vol. 1*, New York: Cosimo.

John, Gus (1976), *The New Black Presence in Britain: A Christian Scrutiny*, London: Community and Race Relations Unit of the British Council of Churches.

Kee, A. (2017), *The Rise and Demise of Black Theology*, London: Routledge.

Lartey, E. (1999), 'After Stephen Lawrence', *Black Theology in Britain: A Journal of Contextual Praxis*, 3, pp. 79–91.

Long, C. (1997), 'Perspectives for a Study of African American Religion in the United States', in Timothy Earl Fulop and Albert J. Raboteau (eds), *African-American Religion: Interpretive essays in history and culture*, New York, Routledge.

Newall, V. (1975), 'Black Britain: The Jamaicans and their folklore', *Folklore*, 106(1).

Patterson, O. (1982), *Slavery and Social Death: A Comparative Study*, Cambridge, MA: Harvard University Press.

Reddie, A. (2003), *Nobodies to Somebodies: A Practical Theology for Education and Liberation*, Peterborough: Epworth Press.

Reid-Salmon, D. (2008), book review of A. Reddie, *Black Theology in Transatlantic Dialogue*, *Black Theology: An International Journal*, 6 (1).

Salcuni, S. (2015), 'New frontiers and applications of attachment theory', in *Frontiers in Psychology*, 6(273), https://www.ncbi.nlm.nih.gov/pmc/articles/PMC4356001/ (accessed 30.9.2021).

Selvon, S. (1956), *Lonely Londoners*, London: Penguin Books.

Thurman, H. (1976), *Jesus and the Disinherited*, Boston: Beacon Press.

Thurman. H. (1998), *A Strange Freedom: The Best of Howard Thurman on Religious Experience and Public Life*, W. Fluker and C. Tumber (eds), Boston, MA: Beacon Press.

Van Sertima, I. (1976), *They Came Before Columbus: The African presence in ancient America*, New York: Random House.

Watkins Ali, C. (1999), *Survival and Liberation: Pastoral Theology in African American Context*, St Louis, MO: Chalice Press.

8

We are Here – Where Next?

This is where we have arrived in our Black British history and in our pastoral theological reflections on how Black people have preserved themselves in terms of their inner musings and sense of community within a Christian framework. There must, if the BMC is to have a viable future in the UK, be a more intentional reaching into the wider community beyond the walls of the religious sanctuary. There are areas requiring further development and on reading this book these will have become very obvious.

1 One of the unheard voices in this book has been Black British women Christians, who have much to ask and say within and without the safety of the walls of the church. In reality, given BMC's composition of 75 per cent women, it is unwise not to include their voices in the further development of a Black British pastoral theology. To use a familiar phrase describing women as 'the backbone of the church', not to include them in the dialogue produces a Black pastoral theology with very little teeth, myopic, pastorally and theologically anaemic and, of course, spineless!

2 A Black British pastoral theology must explore Black Britons as multiple communities with regard to ethnicity (Afro-Caribbean, African immigrant, UK-born) and the different experiences of women and men across these ethnicities. Further pastoral conversations needed to meet this challenge include how pastors can care for people within their congregations when there are a mix of continental Africans and Caribbean people. The current societal reference to Black, Asian and Minority Ethnic, politically known as BAME,

does not mean the same; there are many cosmological nuances where differences are concerned. While there is, it seems, an unspoken societal pressure for homogeneity and assimilation, how are pastors to respond to this smorgasbord of language, culture, heritage and history, with each group having a different understanding of the world, yet loving the same God? This is even before one considers the effects of the legacy of slavery on African Caribbean people, where the effect of intergenerational trauma is no longer considered a figment of their imagination, but understood from the emerging field of neuroscience and epigenetics.

3 A Black British pastoral theology must also create space for the various constructions of Black British identity, in conversation with Black British Christian identity and in the light of different Black British Christian communities (Pentecostal, Anglican, Baptist, Methodist, Seventh-Day Adventist, Catholic, etc.). At present, there is no one voice which speaks for the multitude of Black Christians who worship as part of the various traditions of Christendom within the UK, although there is the One People Commission within the Evangelical Alliance with its strapline of 'The gathering together of God's one church in all its vibrant expressions, modelling the unity of God's people'. While this is a worthwhile initiative, one wonders how much marginalized voices are empowered to speak and whether they will be listened to. Within the Evangelical Alliance there is a separate and unique South Asian Forum. For some, this call for a separate and unique entity may be seen as divisive, because many, despite their discomfort, unrest and difficulty in talking about race, do not want to upset the apple cart. Yet there remains an irony. At a relational level, friendships transcend church and doctrinal differences. This is evidenced at funerals, where the community gathers together out of respect for the deceased and to support their family. Furthermore, if someone is sick within the community, whether they are part of the church or not, prayers are said across the range of Christian traditions inviting God to intervene on their behalf.

4 A Black British pastoral theology must create a space for dialogue between Black British Christianity and the portrayal of Black people in the media, fiction and film. Too often Black British Christianity is silent on many issues, and media, fiction and film are among them. To be sure, there is much conversation behind closed doors, around the dinner table and so forth, but it is seldom that issues are confronted head-on publicly, and even more rarely do you hear sermons that thoughtfully offer a theological response to the depiction of Black people in the media and how God might want Black Christians to respond through the lens of the gospel.

5 A Black British pastoral theology is by nature political, because it deals with the lives of people. In this regard a Black British pastoral theology cannot afford to neglect how power and class shape the life outcomes of Black British Christians. One way in which a Black British pastoral theology could explore those issues is to examine disparities in lifespan, health, education, wealth and so on, between Black and White Britons, as well as between Black Britons of different income brackets. The factors reinforcing racism are much deeper than the colour of one's skin. Within Britain, as well as the USA, many people have undergone unconscious bias training which for many has now proved ineffective. Another step towards looking at issues of race and discrimination is cultural competence. While this has its place, it does not deal effectively with the structural issues of discrimination which affect people on a personal level.

In considering social disparities, what has shocked many parts of the nation is the high number of people from ethnic minority communities who succumbed to the Covid19 pandemic. It was so stark that the government could no longer ignore such disparities. In simple terms, Covid19 exposed fissures and cracks of social inequalities in British society in all their painful rawness. Tackling disparities might be a more objective way of dealing with the sensitivity of race, although the language in vogue is 'diversity', which serves as a general catch-all for differences in society. This term is problematic because it circumvents thorny issues around power, class, stereotypes, prejudices, bias, justice, equality and inclusion. The more recent studies carried out on the ethnic and gender pay gap within the NHS and institutions of higher learning are examples of how such disparity still exists within a culture of Equality, Diversity and Inclusion. The question must be asked, given the fact these are not new findings, why is the gap continuing to exist when many know it is clearly wrong?

Coupled with the ethnic pay gap, another challenge for a Black pastoral theology is to ask why, after all these years, there is still a high attainment gap among minority groups within many British universities.

6 A Black pastoral theology must seriously contend with the thorny issue of human sexuality in all its various expressions. On this matter, there is a long way to go. Many Black Christians are clear on their stance on homosexuality, yet are lacking in understanding of basic human sexuality and how it is a gift from God. In this regard, there is a mountain of work to be done within a context where the lines of sexuality and sexual freedom are in many cases contentiously blurred.

7 Given the complexity of modern life, Black pastoral leadership training is now a must and any church group or pastor who feels that all one needs is the Spirit will have a limited shelf life. This is by no means a recent problem. Similarly, congregations require training that extends beyond the Sunday school, which still exists in some BMCs. The continual development of pastors must be a non-negotiable area of their ministry and they must see themselves as educators, those who empower, teach, instruct, disciple and who have an entrepreneurial outlook while being firmly grounded in the world of biblical theology.

8 A Black British pastoral theology must never break its pastoral neck to find acceptance within the halls of White academia. While it is not a theology that encourages racial separatism, it cannot afford to settle comfortably within the guild while its Black people continue to suffer and their

voices of pain are muted. Black pain must still express itself. In the words of Zora Neale Hurston, 'If you are silent about your pain, they'll kill you and say you enjoyed it.'[1]

9 The final area for a Black British pastoral theology, and Black theology generally, to wrestle with is the nature and expression of love in spite of living within a context of oppression and discrimination. A love which not only considers one's oppression, but bears in mind and understands that while there are the oppressed and oppressors, there are no winners. All suffer because we have fallen woefully short of what God has called us to be and how he wants us to be in a real world.

Questions for further reflection

1 On reading this seminal book, where do you see areas needing further development?

2 While you read this book were there areas in which you felt uncomfortable? If so, what have you decided to do to explore why you felt uncomfortable? Remember that emotions are data and are informing us that something in our lives needs our attention.

Note

1 Quoted in I. Session, K. Sharpe and J. Aldredge-Clanton (2020), *The Gathering: A Womanist Church, Origins, Stories, Sermons and Litanies*, Eugene, OR: Wipf and Stock Publishers, p. 102.

Index of Bible References

Index of Names and Subjects